LUTHERAN MUSIC AND MEANING

■

DANIEL ZAGER

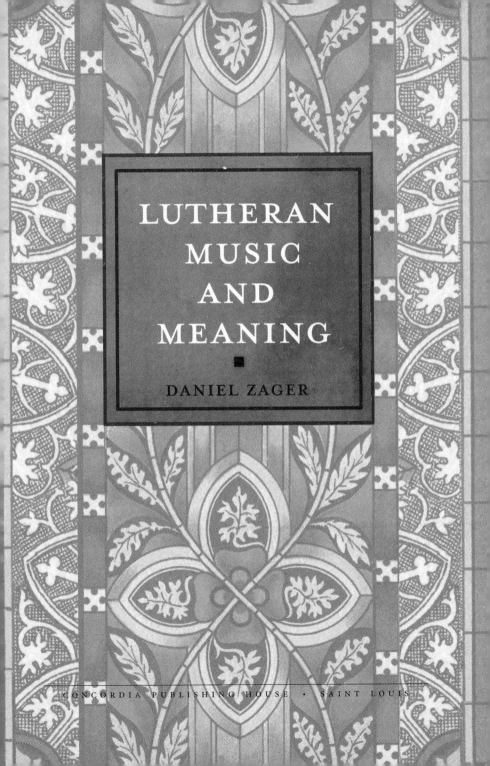

LUTHERAN MUSIC AND MEANING

DANIEL ZAGER

CONCORDIA PUBLISHING HOUSE · SAINT LOUIS

Published by Concordia Publishing House
3558 S. Jefferson Ave., St. Louis, MO 63118-3968
1-800-325-3040 • cph.org

Manufactured in the United States of America

1 2 3 4 5 6 7 8 9 10   32 31 30 29 28 27 26 25 24 23

CONTENTS

Preface   9

Abbreviations   12

Introduction   15

1. Does Lutheran Music Have Meaning?
   The Case of Hymn Tunes and Their Texts   19

   Text, Music, and Meaning in Hymns   23

   Contexts for Meaning in Lutheran Music   30

   Summary   32

2. Luther and Hymns for the Congregation   33

   1523: "The People Could Sing during Mass"   37

   1524: The First Printed Hymn Collections   41

   Summary   50

3. Music for Voices and Instruments in the Lutheran Service:
   What Does It Mean?   53

   Michael Praetorius   56

   Johann Sebastian Bach   62

   Bach: Organ Chorale Preludes   63

   Bach: *Gottes Zeit ist die allerbeste Zeit* (BWV 106)   67

   Bach: *St. Matthew Passion* (Opening Chorus)   75

   Summary   77

4. Liturgy, Church Year, and Lectionary as
   Contexts for Meaning   79

   Music as an Integrated Part of the Divine Service:
   Two Views from the Nineteenth Century   81

   Liturgy—The Divine Service   84

   Church Year   89

   Lectionary   91

   Summary   95

5. Singing and Listening in the Divine Service   97
    Singing   100
    Listening   103
    Theology of Worship → Theology of Music   108
    Summary   110

PREFACE

Why would one take the time to think about, talk about, or write about *meaning* in church music? Isn't meaning just a matter of what the words say? Isn't it sufficient just to sing the hymns and listen to whatever music happens to be included in any given worship service? Moreover, isn't meaning determined by each individual for him- or herself?

Often, the assumption is that while the words—texts of hymns or vocal/choral music—mean exactly what they say, the music itself must be neutral because, unlike words, music doesn't say anything specifically. That line of thinking assumes that music is merely like a tablecloth or a place mat—something that holds the nourishment of the feast but does not in itself contribute to that nourishing feast. I want to explore that issue in this book.

Many Lutherans would find a spoken worship service—without any music at all—to be quite foreign to both past experience and current expectations. But the idea that music should somehow be related—perhaps even tightly related—to the spoken parts of the service, so that music contributes to an integrated whole, is not necessarily expected. I also want to explore that idea in this book.

This book is *not* about how music might be *meaningful* to an individual on an emotional level, how music might relate to or affect an individual's feelings. Indeed, it would be impossible to account for the individual emotional responses of even a small group of people gathered for worship. Moreover, how their varied emotions relate to a particular musical expression on one Sunday, in one season or year, might vary on another similar occasion, for emotions and feelings are fleeting and can and do change over time. While agreeing that meaning in Lutheran music is closely related to, even prompted by, verbal texts, I want to explore how the music itself plays a parallel role to text and can be studied objectively in terms of meaning.

Finally, exploring meaning in Lutheran music becomes a vantage point for probing and further understanding the purpose, significance, and value of music in worship. It provides a way to think about how Lutheran music plays its part in the proclamation of the Gospel.

While there is an extensive body of writing for the benefit of Lutheran church musicians—organists, choir directors, kantors—there is much less for those who make up our congregations. This book is intended primarily for congregational singers and listeners of Lutheran church music.

I extend my deepest thanks to two friends for their assistance with this book. Richard C. Resch read an early draft and provided valued advice, his vast knowledge and experience as a Lutheran kantor and seminary faculty member having shaped my thinking since I first met him in the late 1990s. Every author should be as fortunate as I have been in having a knowledgeable and collegial editor. Peter C. Reske, senior editor of music/worship at Concordia Publishing House, is a longtime friend, and it has been a privilege to collaborate with him on this project, his academic training in musicology and his experience with Lutheran music making him the ideal partner. While acknowledging the assistance of these two colleagues, it is important to state that errors or shortcomings in the book are solely my responsibility. Finally, I thank my wife, Kathy, fellow singer and listener, who has always supported my work as a musicologist and Lutheran musician.

ABBREVIATIONS

AE   *Luther's Works: American Edition.* 82 vols. St. Louis: Concordia Publishing House; Philadelphia/Minneapolis: Muhlenberg/Fortress Press, 1955–.

BWV   *Bach-Werke-Verzeichnis. Thematisch-systematisches Verzeichnis der musikalischen Werke von Johann Sebastian Bach.* Edited by Wolfgang Schmieder. 2nd expanded ed. Wiesbaden: Breitkopf & Härtel, 1990.

CW93   *Christian Worship: A Lutheran Hymnal.* Milwaukee: Northwestern Publishing House, 1993.

CW21   *Christian Worship: Hymnal.* Milwaukee: Northwestern Publishing House, 2021.

EG   *Evangelisches Gesangbuch: Ausgabe für die Evangelisch-Lutherischen Kirchen in Bayern und Thüringen.* München: Evangelischer Presseverband für Bayern; Weimar: Wartburg Verlag, [1995].

ELH   *Evangelical Lutheran Hymnary.* St. Louis: MorningStar Music Publishers, 1996.

ELW   *Evangelical Lutheran Worship.* Minneapolis: Augsburg Fortress, 2006.

Jenny   Markus Jenny, *Luthers geistliche Lieder und*

Kirchengesänge: Vollständige Neuedition in Ergänzung zu Band 35 der Weimarer Ausgabe. Archiv zur Weimarer Ausgabe der Werke Martin Luthers, Texte und Untersuchungen, Band 4. Köln, Wien: Böhlau Verlag, 1985.

LBW *Lutheran Book of Worship.* Minneapolis: Augsburg Publishing House, 1978.

LSB *Lutheran Service Book.* St. Louis: Concordia Publishing House, 2006.

LSB-CH *Lutheran Service Book: Companion to the Hymns.* Edited by Joseph Herl, Peter C. Reske, and Jon D. Vieker. 2 vols. St. Louis: Concordia Publishing House, 2019.

LW *Lutheran Worship.* St. Louis: Concordia Publishing House, 1982.

PraeSM I Michael Praetorius, *Syntagma Musicum* I, trans. Michael D. Fleming, "Michael Praetorius, Music Historian: An Annotated Translation of 'Syntagma Musicum' I, Part 1" (PhD diss., Washington University in St. Louis, 1979).

TLH *The Lutheran Hymnal.* St. Louis: Concordia Publishing House, 1941.

WOV *With One Voice: A Lutheran Resource for Worship.* Minneapolis: Augsburg Fortress, 1995.

INTRODUCTION

In Martin Luther's Small Catechism (1529), each of his explanatory comments is prefaced by the question "*Was ist das?*" ("What is this?"). The English version of the catechism that I used as an elementary school student translated the question a bit more freely: "What does this mean?" Since this book is concerned with questions of *meaning* in Lutheran music, I borrow that concise yet profound question as a central focus for this book. What—if anything—does Lutheran music mean? In fact, can *music* (composed of nonverbal pitches and rhythms) take on meaning? If so, how? More precisely for this inquiry, can Lutheran music convey, indicate, or signal theological meaning? If so, how does that happen, and what categories of church music might do so: congregational hymns, vocal and choral music, organ or other instrumental music?

Of course, an obvious answer to such questions is that meaning in Lutheran music derives from associated theological *texts*, for example, the texts of congregational hymns, or liturgical texts such as the Kyrie ("Lord, have mercy"), the Gloria in Excelsis ("Glory be to God on high"), the Sanctus ("Holy, holy, holy"), the Agnus Dei ("Lamb of God"), the Nunc Dimittis ("Lord, now You let Your servant go in peace"), or the Magnificat ("My soul magnifies the Lord"). Given this omnipresent link between music and texts in

15

Lutheran music, we don't ask merely, "What does the music of a particular hymn mean?" Rather, we explore how that music—hymn tune and setting—participates in *signaling* and conveying the meaning of an associated text (or texts). We ask how the music supports and enhances the *sacred* nature of the text in a way that is distinct from the secular culture in which we live. It is in this sense that we consider questions of how Lutheran music takes on meaning—how sacred music appropriately *complements* sacred texts, "sacred" indicating musical and textual expressions that are set apart to be employed appropriately in the Church's worship.

To use a single brief example: when we sing "Praise God, from Whom All Blessings Flow" (*LSB* 805) to the well-known tune OLD HUNDREDTH, we draw on music that is distinct from the secular culture, music that won't be heard at a rock or country western concert, or at the halftime extravaganza of the Super Bowl, or in connection with television advertising. Such sacred music grows out of the varied historical cultures and epochs of the Western Church, ranging from the monophonic, or "Gregorian", chant of the Early Church (monophonic = only one vocal line), to the vast repertory of fifteenth- and sixteenth-century polyphonic sacred music (polyphonic = two or more vocal lines), to the chorales (hymns) of the Lutheran Reformation, the metrical psalm tunes (like OLD HUNDREDTH) of the Calvinist strain of the Reformation, the sacred cantatas of J. S. Bach, and on and on through the Church's vast and rich musical history.

How does music intended for Lutheran worship differ from, say, Western art music (or "classical" music) heard in concert halls and opera houses, or from concerts by jazz, rock, or country musicians? Sacred music in the Lutheran tradition has long been characterized by a *proclamatory function*—music playing its role in proclaiming the Gospel. Unlike in a concert, music in the Lutheran Divine Service (or *Gottesdienst* = "God's service to us") is never merely music for the sake of music, or music for the sake of art. Luther himself articulated this proclamatory function of music:

> After all, the gift of language combined with the gift of song was only given to man to let him know that he should praise God with both word and music, namely, by proclaiming [the Word of God] through music and by providing sweet melodies with words. (AE 53:323–24; brackets in original)

Luther's drawing together of words and music established the foundation for the proclamatory role of music in Lutheran worship and the necessity for music to complement the meaning of texts, thus for music to take on a textually dependent theological meaning of its own. Related to questions of meaning are questions of *identity*: how might church music contribute to a distinctly Lutheran identity? Does music play a role—along with liturgy, preaching, and creedal and confessional statements—in establishing Lutheran identity?

It is important to clarify at the outset what I mean by the phrase "Lutheran music." By that phrase, I refer to the distinctive living heritage of music composed intentionally (or borrowed/adapted) from the sixteenth century to the present day for use within the

LUTHERAN MUSIC AND MEANING

Lutheran Divine Service and the Office hours (Matins, Vespers, and Compline). Of first importance, I include hymn melodies and settings for congregational singing; secondarily, music composed for choirs and for instruments, with particular emphasis on music for the organ, which during the first half of the seventeenth century began to assume a prominence in Lutheran worship that continues to our own time. As living Lutheran composers write well-crafted, hymn-based compositions for the organ, thus continuing this rich genre of Lutheran music, they are also finding new potentials in hymn-based compositions for the piano, thus enlarging the possibilities of keyboard music for the Church.

While this book is for all who have an interest in Lutheran music, it is intended especially for the singers and listeners who make up Lutheran congregations. Thus, it is not a history of Lutheran music, though it makes use of that history to examine questions of meaning in Lutheran music. Nor is it a "how-to" handbook for Lutheran kantors, organists, and choir directors who lead music in Lutheran congregations, some of whom have no doubt pondered these same questions as a part of their own work. My goal is simply to explore questions of how Lutheran music might have the capacity to convey theological meaning to the singers and listeners in our congregations. My presupposition is that Lutheran music does indeed have that capacity, which is why composers from Martin Luther on have created hymn tunes for congregational singers, and why composers from Luther's day to our time in the twenty-first century have provided a rich legacy of vocal/choral and instrumental music.

CHAPTER 1

DOES LUTHERAN MUSIC HAVE MEANING?

The Case of Hymn Tunes and Their Texts

Browsing in the University of North Carolina at Chapel Hill bookstore in 1999, I came across a then recently published volume by Nicholas Cook entitled *Music: A Very Short Introduction*. It didn't take long for this book to stimulate my thinking, for on only the second page of his foreword the author wrote:

> To talk about music in general is to talk about what music means—and more basically, how it is (how it can be) that music operates as an agent of meaning. For music isn't just something nice to listen to. On the contrary, it's deeply embedded in human culture.[1]

A large part of my musical identity was (and remains) that of Lutheran organist and church musician, so I began to apply Cook's statements to my small corner of the larger musical world that he was exploring. What about the organ music I played each Sunday at a Lutheran church in nearby Durham, North Carolina—what does it mean? Does it mean anything at all to my fellow congregants?

---

1   Nicholas Cook, *Music: A Very Short Introduction* (New York: Oxford University Press, 1998), vi.

Or is it "just something nice to listen to"? How might the music at a Sunday morning worship service take on meaning? And how might such music be "deeply embedded" in a particular "culture," such as that of the Lutheran Church at worship in late twentieth-century America?

Cook's statement prompted my thinking about such questions, and, in truth, it nagged at me, for this was not the first occasion for me to ponder such basic, underlying concerns related to my vocation as a Lutheran church musician. As an undergraduate organ performance major at the University of Wisconsin–Madison, I was fortunate indeed to be the organist for a Lutheran student congregation for five years, and for four of those years to work with a pastor, the Rev. Dr. Wayne E. Schmidt, who was himself a fine organist and church musician (who would, subsequent to his work as campus pastor, become a faculty member at Concordia Seminary, St. Louis). We had wonderful, extensive conversations about Lutheran music, and I likely made him late for dinner with his family on more than one occasion. He helped me to refine my thinking about the purpose of music in Lutheran worship, and I remember that on walks back to my apartment, I would continue to try to work out in my mind questions regarding the function and purpose of music in Lutheran worship—existential questions for one who wished to devote his life to Lutheran music.

In graduate school at the University of Minnesota, I was fortunate to have a position as organist at a Lutheran church in suburban Minneapolis. There I was invited to do occasional teaching in the context of Sunday morning adult classes. At one point, I decided to explore some of these questions with my fellow congregants. One Sunday in January, we met in the organ and choir balcony so that I could play, as an example for our discussion, Andreas Armsdorff's (1670–99) setting of the chorale "Wie schön leuchtet der Morgenstern," the Epiphany hymn "O Morning Star, How Fair and Bright" (*LSB* 395). I purposely chose this setting because the hymn melody was unornamented and could be heard prominently; it was a hymn familiar to this congregation, and the melody in Armsdorff's chorale prelude couldn't be missed by those listeners. I suggested that an appropriate way to listen to such an organ prelude at the beginning of a worship service would be to read the text in the hymnal as I played the composition—the text being what prompted the composer to write this setting, the hymn text thus lending a particular *meaning* to this musical composition. The next Sunday, one of those congregants told me that he did precisely that, and the organ prelude at the beginning of the service took on new meaning for him. I was thrilled because music, hymn text, and theology had coalesced in a meaningful way for that listener—at least on that one occasion.

That welcome response aside, problems remained with regard to my thinking on the role and function of music in Lutheran worship—problems for the church musician and for the listener. From the standpoint of the Lutheran musician: while I continue to prefer organ music with clearly audible hymn tune references for the worship service, such compositions are not always available. And perhaps such choices are not always desirable, since organ preludes with ornamented or somewhat disguised hymn tune references still merit a place among musical settings chosen for the worship service. From the standpoint of the Lutheran congregant: not all listeners have the familiarity—gained over years of hymn singing—to link a hymn melody to its associated text and then to the theological content of that text (even when the hymnic basis of an organ setting is referenced in the printed Sunday bulletin). Even more to the point, not all listeners have the desire for such active listening in worship services. Does that mean that music in Lutheran worship might be, contrary to Cook's point, "just something nice to listen to," or music that sets a mood, or, as some might say, something that (vaguely) "prepares the heart for worship"? To settle for such a premise would be to deny historic Lutheran propositions that music is a means of Gospel proclamation (about which, more in the following chapters). Does that proposition require our congregants to take a course in Lutheran music appreciation? That is emphatically not the case, nor is it the purpose of this book; rather, I simply wish to heighten awareness of the potential of Lutheran music to participate in the proclamation of the Gospel. That such a premise may suggest a need for active listening is hardly anomalous, for worship does require effort: to focus, to think, to concentrate, to learn, to pay attention to God's Word. That is true for Scripture readings, for the pastor's sermon, for the prayers, for the liturgy, and for church music in all its varied forms—whether sung by the congregation, chanted by the pastor, sung by a choir, or played on the organ or other instruments.

Text, Music, and Meaning in Hymns

Contrary to Cook's premise "that music operates as an agent of meaning," there are many in the Church who believe that meaning derives only from verbal texts, that music is neutral, and that its pitches and rhythms do not contribute to or convey meaning. As an example, consider this statement from Rick Warren:

> Music is nothing more than an arrangement of notes and rhythms; it's the words that make a song spiritual. . . . If I were to play a tune for you without any words, you wouldn't know if it was a Christian song or not.[2]

Lutheran pastors who agree with such a statement know that they can evaluate verbal texts on the basis of Scripture and the Lutheran Confessions, thereby permitting doctrinal judgments about hymn texts or the words of vocal/choral music. There is, however, no parallel or similar evaluative process for the pitches and rhythms of musical compositions. Some Lutheran pastors have concluded, therefore, that music is neutral and that any type or style of music can be used in the Divine Service—so long as the texts are not in error when measured against Scripture and the Confessions. Moreover, it's probably not far off the mark to acknowledge that many singers and listeners in Lutheran congregations would agree.

Let's consider the second part of Warren's quotation: "If I were to play a tune for you without any words, you wouldn't know if it

---

2   Rick Warren, *The Purpose Driven Church: Growth without Compromising Your Message and Mission* (Grand Rapids, MI: Zondervan, 1995), 281.

was a Christian song or not." To be precise, he means a tune without either a sung text or an implied text such as with "Yankee Doo-
dle," which, even if the words aren't sung, has a tune that by itself is
sufficient to bring those words to mind for the average American
listener. In thinking specifically here about hymns, we can look at
Example 1 below, which shows a melody without any text—actual
or implied. It has the characteristics of a hymn tune, and it could
accommodate a text such as "O God, My Faithful God" (*LSB* 696)
or "Now Thank We All Our God" (*LSB* 895). But, in fact, it is wedded to no known hymn text; it is simply a stand-alone melody—in
this case, one I wrote to demonstrate Warren's point. What does
this melody mean? One could sing or play the melody to become
familiar with it. One could evaluate the melodic contour of this
melody and the harmonic implications of the melodic phrases.
One could critique the musical construction of this melody. But

Example 1

such musical matters, important as they may be, do not shed any light on the meaning of this hymn melody. In fact, this melody, by itself, conveys no theological meaning. If it is to be a hymn melody, it needs an associated hymn text or *texts*, for in hymnody it is often *not* the case that a given melody consistently bears a one-to-one relationship with only a single hymn text. As we shall see, however, that circumstance does not negate the fact that a well-composed (or appropriately borrowed) hymn melody has the capacity—even when coupled with multiple texts—to signal theological meaning.

Consider, for example, the wonderful hymn tune WIE SCHÖN LEUCHTET by the Lutheran pastor Philipp Nicolai (1556–1608). This Epiphany hymn—text and tune both written by Nicolai—has been translated as "O Morning Star, How Fair and Bright" (*LSB* 395) and "How Lovely Shines the Morning Star" (*TLH* 343). But this strong melody has also been joined to other texts such as a one-stanza Christmas hymn by the Danish poet Birgitte Katerine Boye (1742–1824), "Rejoice, Rejoice This Happy Morn" (*LSB* 391); a one-stanza Easter hymn by the same poet, "He Is Arisen! Glorious Word" (*LSB* 488); "Alleluia! Let Praises Ring" (*LSB* 822), which in its 1698 publication specified the melody WIE SCHÖN LEUCHTET (*LSB-CH* 1:1247); and "O Holy Spirit, Enter In" (*LSB* 913), which in its 1640 publication specified the same melody (*LSB-CH* 1:1460). While this tune retains a primary theological meaning relating to its original Epiphany text by poet-composer Nicolai, it has been appropriately joined to these other texts, all of which sound some of the same theological notes of praise and adoration found in the initial 1599 text by Nicolai.

But now to Warren's first point: "Music is nothing more than an arrangement of notes and rhythms." This is demonstrably false. Why? Because in church music, especially with congregational hymns, we don't encounter the kind of melody shown in Example 1, which has no known relationship to any hymn text. Hymn melodies sung in Christian congregations, and printed in Christian hymnals, are connected with texts and—to use Cook's apt phrase—are subsequently "deeply embedded" in Christian cultures of sung theology. As congregational singers, we *learn* these text/music relationships over time, and they become "deeply embedded" in our memories.

Consider the well-known melody for the Christmas carol "Silent Night." Once connected with that text, the melody becomes more than "an arrangement of notes and rhythms." The melody itself conveys meaning; it signifies the feast of Christmas, more particularly perhaps, Christmas Eve worship. Music + text = meaning. It would be foolish to think that this melody is neutral and, therefore, could work equally well on Easter morning, to accommodate this text:

> Jesus is raised from the dead.
> Now He lives, as He said.
> Crucified upon a cross,
> When it seemed that all was loss,
>> Christ is risen today,
>> Christ is risen today.

Franz Gruber's melody is inextricably linked to Joseph Mohr's Christmas text, learned by Christian singers the world over.

The pitches and rhythms of this melody have taken on meaning by virtue of the text for which it was composed. Text + music = meaning. Moreover, even without a text, the melody of "Silent Night," with its gentle rocking motion, is unlikely to suggest itself as a suitable melody for a newly written Easter text. Nor would the melody for "Christ the Lord Is Risen Today; Alleluia" (*LSB* 463), with its rising fanfare-like gestures, necessarily be an obvious choice to accommodate a Christmas Eve hymn text. It is not true that "music is nothing more than an arrangement of notes and rhythms," for in our hymns and hymnals, we don't encounter textless tunes. Rather, texts confer meaning on their associated hymn melodies, and congregational singers and listeners assimilate and learn those connections and meanings over a lifetime of singing the faith.

Hymn melodies are not only the most straightforward and concise musical expressions within Lutheran worship but, arguably, the most important, for the congregational hymn is where the assembled singers and listeners of the congregation join to play their part in proclaiming the Gospel and in "worship[ing] one God in Trinity and Trinity in Unity" (Athanasian Creed 4; *LSB*, p. 319). The meaning of Lutheran hymns derives not only from their texts but also from the music. The *sound* of the music will play an important role in either *complementing* the sacred nature of the hymn text or *competing against* that text by introducing musical sounds, gestures, and genres rooted in the secular cultures around us. Hymns are such *concise* theological, poetic, and musical expressions, and in any consideration of meaning, the musical dimension of a hymn must not be neglected, however difficult that evaluation may be—compared to the more straightforward textual (both theological and poetic) dimensions of Christian hymnody.

If text + music = meaning, then it is not just a matter of judging a hymn based on its text; the music, too, contributes to its meaning. While the musical pitches and rhythms will indeed play a part in signaling meaning, by themselves they are insufficient to establish full theological meaning. Thus, for its meaning, a hymn melody is contingent in part on a hymn text, but the equally important parallel proposition is that the hymn text needs to be coupled with a melody that complements and supports it, without suggesting or evoking nontheological meanings alien to that text.

Consider the hymn text "O Christ the Same" by Timothy Dudley-Smith (1926–). The 1995 hymnal supplement *With One Voice* coupled that text with the tune LONDONDERRY AIR (*WOV* 778), an Irish folk tune bearing significant nontheological meaning through its well-known association with the text "Oh, Danny Boy" (written in 1910). When the 2006 hymnal *Evangelical Lutheran Worship* was compiled, Dudley-Smith's text was paired with a new tune and setting by Carl Schalk (1929–2021), RED HILL ROAD (*ELW* 760), which fits the text well and avoids connection with a secular tune that continues to bear its own associative meanings. Paul Westermeyer offers the following insightful commentary on LONDONDERRY AIR:

> Though not a bad tune, it poses vocal and associative problems for an assembly at worship: it is a solo venture of an octave and fifth, not a communal vocal

endeavor; and its tie to "Oh, Danny Boy" and a dead lover's grave may pull at the heart strings but superimpose fantasy on truth.[3]

LISTENING: Listen to Dudley-Smith's text "O Christ the Same" sung to Schalk's tune RED HILL ROAD on YouTube by searching "O Christ the Same, ELW 760, Mount Olive Lutheran."

Thus, in a congregational hymn, musical meaning will be understood in part by whether the melody has extratheological associative meanings that continue to be familiar to congregational singers, or whether the melody derives from the Church's own creative culture and supports the text without introducing conflicting meanings. That creative culture for Lutherans begins in the 1520s with Luther and his co-workers composing new tunes and extends to living Lutheran composers of our own day.

In addition to music *composed* for Lutheran worship, hymn melodies have sometimes been *borrowed* from secular repertories of the Western *art music* tradition; prominent composers such as Heinrich Isaac (ca. 1450/55–1517), Hans Leo Hassler (1564–1612), and Gustav Holst (1874–1934) come readily to mind. Secular melodies by these composers have been judiciously borrowed to accommodate sacred hymn texts. Isaac's secular song "Innsbruck, ich muss dich lassen" is used for three hymns in *LSB*: the Epiphany hymn "Arise and Shine in Splendor" (*LSB* 396), the hymn for Holy Week "Upon the Cross Extended" (*LSB* 453), and the evening

3   Paul Westermeyer, *Hymnal Companion to Evangelical Lutheran Worship* (Minneapolis: Augsburg Fortress, 2010), 621–22.

29

hymn "Now Rest beneath Night's Shadow" (*LSB* 880). Hassler's art song, "Mein gmüth ist mir verwirret", provides the well-known melody for "O Sacred Head, Now Wounded" (*LSB* 450 and 449). Holst's melody, known as THAXTED, is drawn from the "Jupiter" movement of his orchestral work *The Planets*, and in *LSB* accommodates Stephen Starke's paraphrase of the Te Deum laudamus, "We Praise You and Acknowledge You, O God" (*LSB* 941).

Moreover, Lutheran hymnals borrow hymn texts, melodies, and settings from the distinctive repertories and heritages of various Christian denominations and hymnals, as well as music from a variety of folk and ethnic traditions. Of course, that raises the question of why not utilize the Irish folk tune discussed earlier? An essential consideration is that of an appropriate *distance of time* between (1) the original contexts and the well-known, common uses of that folk tune and (2) its inclusion in hymnals. While LONDONDERRY AIR is not sufficiently distant from its connection to "Oh, Danny Boy," there are other Irish folk tunes that carry no such associative meanings for the twenty-first-century American listener; see, for example, the tune MOVILLE, an Irish folk tune used for the hymn text "Christ Is the World's Redeemer" (LSB 539).

LISTENING: Listen to the tune MOVILLE on YouTube by searching "Moville hymn tune."

CONTEXTS FOR MEANING IN LUTHERAN MUSIC

These brief case studies of hymn melodies demonstrate that meaning in Lutheran music is contingent, or dependent, on factors other than the purely musical. The contexts for probing meaning in Lutheran music—not only in hymns but also in vocal/choral and instrumental music of all kinds—involve the following factors:

- Theological and poetic **texts**.

- The historic **liturgy** of the Western Church, which is the overall framework for music in Lutheran worship.

- The **Church Year** as a means of organizing and defining time through the annual cycle of feasts centering on God's redemptive work in Christ.

- A **lectionary** as a means of organizing and specifying scriptural content for each feast or day in the Church Year.

- **Historic** Lutheran **musical repertories**, which not only continue to provide content for Lutheran worship but also establish standards of musical craftsmanship and liturgical functionality, thus furnishing examples for newly composed music in our present culture of Lutheran worship.

Thus, the meaning of music in Lutheran worship depends on this complex web of contextual factors: (1) how the music supports an actual or implied text, (2) how the musical plus textual expression finds its place in the liturgy, (3) how that expression fits into and supports both Church Year and lectionary, and (4) how the music connects with the standards and patterns established by the long history of music composed (or borrowed) for use in Lutheran liturgical worship.

SUMMARY

In Lutheran worship—whether the Divine Service or the Offices of Matins, Vespers, and Compline—music plays a prominent role. Whether that music is sung by the congregation, chanted by the pastor, sung by a vocal or choral ensemble, or played on instruments, the music, in Cook's words, "operates as an agent of meaning." There are, however, no compositional guidelines or recipes that specify for the composer how to establish certain meanings or indeed tell the listener how to discern those meanings. But that reality does not inevitably result in a kind of simplistic relativism that concludes only that an infinite number of meanings may reside in the ears and minds of multiple listeners. Lutheran music exists in a rich contextual web of theology and liturgy, based in the long-standing (from Luther on) expectation that music in the Lutheran liturgy will, in fact, be the sung proclamation of the Gospel. Of course, such music is coupled with actual or implied verbal texts, but that fact never denies the nonverbal power of music to convey and enhance theological meanings deeply rooted in the Christian Gospel. The chapters that follow explore the expectation that Lutheran music is more than an expression of beauty, that it does indeed operate as an agent of theological meaning in the service of Gospel proclamation—both in the case of congregational hymns as well as music composed for choirs and for instruments.

CHAPTER 2

LUTHER AND HYMNS FOR THE CONGREGATION

At the outset, it is important to dispel two related myths about Martin Luther and hymns for the congregation to sing. First, there is no evidence for the assertion that Luther "took tunes that were sung in bars and wrote God-inspired words to go along with the melodies."[4] This myth, propagated by numerous writers to suggest that Luther willingly borrowed from the popular culture of his time, may find its roots in a simple misunderstanding of the German musical term "*Barform*." Bar form is a three-part form—expressed AAB—in which the initial music (A) is repeated (A) before moving on to new music (B). A bar form chorale (or hymn) melody is one that shows this kind of repetition, thus making it easier for a singing congregation to assimilate a melody by ear. An example of a bar form chorale is Luther's melody for "A Mighty Fortress Is Our God" (*LSB* 656). The melody for

> A mighty fortress is our God,
> A trusty shield and weapon;

is subsequently repeated for the next two poetic lines:

> He helps us free from ev'ry need
> That hath us now o'ertaken.

---

4   Walt Kallestad, *Entertainment Evangelism: Taking the Church Public* (Nashville: Abingdon, 1996), 10.

Thus, a single melodic phrase is used twice (AA) before moving on to new melodic material (B), starting with the text "The old evil foe" and proceeding to the end of the poetic stanza. The repetition in a bar form chorale—AAB—facilitates congregational singing of a hymn melody; having learned the first phrase, the singers can confidently repeat it before moving on to new musical phrases. The melodies of bar form chorales have nothing to do with bars or taverns and whatever songs might have been transmitted orally in the popular culture. In fact, Luther, who was musically knowledgeable and proficient, composed this melody specifically for his text "A Mighty Fortress."

A second, related myth supposes that Luther asked: "Why should the devil have all the good tunes?" Again, the intent is to show Luther's openness to the popular music of his day. But there is no evidence in his voluminous writings, including his informal conversations at the dinner table (many of which were written down by his associates), that Luther ever said those words. The quotation is correctly attributed to the English clergyman the Rev. Rowland Hill (1744–1833).[5] While Luther did draw on folk-song repertories, the notion that he borrowed drinking songs from taverns, or that he might have sanctioned bawdy song melodies (the "devil's tunes"), is unsupported by facts or evidence. To the contrary, in his preface to Johann Walter's (1496–1570) 1524 collection of hymn settings for choir, Luther had this to say about the popular music of his day:

---

5   John Bartlett, *Familiar Quotations*, 11th ed. (Boston: Little, Brown, 1937), 274. See also James L. Brauer, "The Devil's Tunes," *Concordia Journal* 23, no. 1 (January 1997): 2–3.

> And these songs [i.e., Walter's settings] were arranged in four parts to give the young—who should at any rate be trained in music and other fine arts—something to wean them away from love ballads and carnal songs and to teach them something of value in their place. (AE 53:316)

These words are clearly not the words of one who would accommodate the popular music of his time for newly composed hymn texts.

In fact, Luther's melody for "From Heaven Above to Earth I Come" (*LSB* 358) provides an interesting case in point. This Christmas hymn, "Vom Himmel hoch, da komm ich her," takes as an initial point of departure the similarly titled folk song "Ich kumm aus frembden landen her" ("I come here from foreign lands"). Luther's first stanza modifies the folk song's picture of an itinerant singer bringing news from a distant place to become more specifically an angel from heaven, who proceeds to tell the good news of the Savior's birth. When this hymn was printed in 1535, it was coupled, logically enough, with the melody traditionally used with the folk song.[6] But when it was printed again only four years later in 1539, it was coupled with a new tune by Luther, the tune that continues to be associated with this text some five centuries later. We can't know with certainty why Luther wrote the new tune. Perhaps, as the writer of the text, he had in mind some melodic ideas that he eventually fashioned into a completed tune. Perhaps he simply didn't want a well-known folk melody to be coupled with his text

---

6   See Jenny, 287, for a notated version of this melody.

as it began to be disseminated more frequently in printed hymnals. What we can conclude is that he clearly was not fully satisfied with his new Christmas text being coupled with an existing secular tune. The situation may have been quite similar to the one mentioned in the previous chapter—the hymn text "O Christ the Same" being sung to the well-known Irish tune LONDONDERRY AIR, whose connection to the secular text "Oh, Danny Boy" is still very much alive and present in the twenty-first century. The same circumstance of a mismatch between sacred text and secular tune might well have been true for Luther, thus prompting his composition of a new tune without preexisting associative meaning, just as Schalk's tune RED HILL ROAD did for Dudley-Smith's text.

It would be fair to say that Luther's tune—composed for this text—*means* something specific, namely, Christmas, the incarnation, the birth of the Savior. This tune has been linked to this text since 1539. We still sing it at Christmas. Composers both well known—such as Michael Praetorius (1571–1621), Johann Pachelbel (1653–1706), and Johann Sebastian Bach (1685–1750)—and less known have provided organ settings and choral versions of this Christmas hymn. *The Lutheran Hymnal* (1941) also assigned this tune to an Advent text by Reginald Heber (1783–1826), "Hosanna to the Living Lord" (*TLH* 70), which I always found puzzling, thinking that the tune is better reserved for Christmas and should not be co-opted a few weeks prior during the Advent season. *Lutheran Service Book* also assigns Luther's tune to another Christmas hymn, the fifth-century Christmas text "A solis ortus cardine," "From East to West" (*LSB* 385). Assessing the meaning of a hymn melody in terms of its theological signification is not always straightforward, for, as we saw in chapter 1 with WIE SCHÖN LEUCHTET, it is not always the case that there is a one-to-one relationship in which a hymn melody is used solely and uniquely with a single hymn text. While for the most part Luther's melody VOM HIMMEL HOCH is used with his corresponding Christmas text, even here there are anomalies of the type just mentioned. To explore further the prospect of meaning in hymn melodies, let's go back to the beginning of Lutheran hymnody, to 1523 with Luther's early stated desire for congregational hymn singing, and to the earliest Lutheran hymnals of 1524.

1523: "THE PEOPLE COULD SING DURING MASS"

In October 1517, Luther wrote his "Disputation on the Power and Efficacy of Indulgences," the document that would come to be known more popularly as the Ninety-Five Theses. By tradition, this work has been understood as a kind of chronological beginning for the Reformation movement in the German-speaking lands. Luther and his colleagues had their work cut out for them on many fronts as the task of reforming the church got underway. Among other pressing matters, Luther was asked to provide guidance on how the Mass should be observed. In 1523, he provided detailed direction for the Latin Mass through his publication of the *Formula Missae* (AE 53:15–40). Luther's outline for observing a German-language Mass would appear three years later in his 1526 *Deutsche Messe* (AE 53:51–90).

Near the end of the *Formula Missae*, Luther expressed his desire to have the people sing hymns in their own language:

> I also wish that we had as many songs as possible in the vernacular which the people could sing during mass, immediately after the gradual and also after the Sanctus and Agnus Dei. For who doubts that originally all the people sang these which now only the choir sings or responds to while the bishop is consecrating? The bishops may have these [congregational] hymns sung either after the Latin chants, or use the Latin on one [Sun]day and the vernacular on the next, until the time comes that the whole mass is sung in the vernacular. But poets are wanting among us, or not yet known, who could compose evangelical and spiritual songs, as Paul calls them [Col. 3:16], worthy to be used in the church of God. . . . For few are found that are written in a proper devotional style. I mention this to encourage any German poets to compose evangelical hymns for us. (AE 53:36–37; brackets in original)

Evidently Luther believed that at some point the Mass would be conducted entirely in the vernacular, though as a transition to that goal, he was quite willing to consider various ways to insert German hymns into the Latin service. Three years later, however, when he published instructions for the German Mass, he clarified his thinking on the continuing use of the Latin language:

Now there are three kinds of divine service or mass.

The first is the one in Latin which we published earlier under the title *Formula Missae*. It is not now my intention to abrogate or to change this service. It shall not be affected in the form which we have followed so far; but we shall continue to use it when or where we are pleased or prompted to do so. For in no wise would I want to discontinue the service in the Latin language, because the young are my chief concern. And if I could bring it to pass, and Greek and Hebrew were as familiar to us as the Latin and had as many fine melodies and songs, we would hold mass, sing, and read on successive Sundays in all four languages, German, Latin, Greek, and Hebrew. I do not at all agree with those who cling to one language and despise all others. (AE 53:62–63)

Retaining the Mass in Latin, as laid out in his *Formula Missae*, would be a means for the young to learn Latin—an important educational goal for Luther.

Nevertheless, the *German Mass and Order of Service* (the *Deutsche Messe*) was necessary according to Luther "for the sake of the unlearned lay folk" (AE 53:63). As he laid out this order of service, he specified German hymns at certain points: (1) "to begin the service we sing a hymn or a German Psalm" (AE 53:69); (2) after the Epistle; (3) "after the Gospel the whole congregation sings the Creed in German: 'In One True God We All Believe' [*LSB* 954]" (AE 53:78); and (4) after the consecration of the elements for the Lord's Supper and during the distribution of the Lord's body and blood. There Luther suggests specifically the Sanctus hymn "Isaiah, Mighty Seer in Days of Old" (*LSB* 960), the Agnus Dei hymn "O Christ, Thou Lamb of God" (*LSB*, p. 198), and the communion hymns "O Lord, We Praise Thee" by Luther himself (*LSB* 617) or "Jesus Christ, Our Blessed Savior" by John Hus (*LSB* 627) (see AE 53:81–82).

From his advocacy of German-language hymns appended to the *Formula Missae*, it is clear that Luther had high literary expectations. He stated that hymns in the German language must be written "in a proper devotional style" and must be "worthy to be used in the church of God." In this part of the *Formula Missae*, he put out a call encouraging German poets to join him in this new undertaking. Further, in late 1523, Luther wrote a letter to his Wittenberg colleague Georg Spalatin (1484–1545), a learned humanist as well as private secretary and court preacher to Elector Frederick III.

> [Our] plan is to follow the example of the prophets and the ancient fathers of the church, and to compose psalms for the people [in the] vernacular, that is, spiritual songs, so that the Word of God may be among the people also in the form of music. Therefore we are searching everywhere for poets. Since you are endowed with a wealth [of knowledge] and elegance [in handling] the German language, and since you have polished [your German] through much use, I ask you to work with us on this project; try to adapt any one of

the psalms for use as a hymn, as you may see [I have done] in this example. But I would like you to avoid any new words or the language used at court. In order to be understood by the people, only the simplest and the most common words should be used for singing; at the same time, however, they should be pure and apt; and further, the sense should be clear and as close as possible to the psalm. (AE 49:68–69; brackets in original)

Here we see Luther getting right to work on his hope for German-language hymns, expressed just a few months earlier in the *Formula Missae*. Along with the letter, he sent an example of his own to Spalatin, perhaps the hymn "From Depths of Woe I Cry to Thee," Luther's paraphrase of Psalm 130 (*LSB* 607). In asking Spalatin for a similar psalm paraphrase, Luther gave him quite the poetic challenge: avoid the highfalutin language used at the ruler's court, but while using simple and common vocabulary, the words needed to be well chosen in order to match the psalm as closely as possible. Of course, Luther is asking Spalatin for a poetic, literary expression, not for a hymn melody, but he makes abundantly clear that the poetry he is seeking is for *singing* "so that the Word of God may be among the people also in the form of music."

1524: THE FIRST PRINTED HYMN COLLECTIONS

By 1524, small booklets of hymns began to be printed, combining into collections hymns that might first have appeared in print as inexpensive single sheets (sometimes referred to as "broadsides"). A superb historical account of Luther's push for German-language congregational hymns, and their earliest publication in the 1520s, may be found in Robin A. Leaver's *The Whole Church Sings*.[7] He explores vernacular song prior to the Reformation as important context for the development of congregational hymns in German, before focusing on hymns and hymnals from 1524 to 1529. In particular, he demonstrates that a hymnal for the laity (*"für die layen"*) appeared as early as 1524 or 1525, establishing that the singing of German-language hymns (chorales) was not the sole province of choirs—even in this first decade of hymn and hymnal development.

Hymnal publications in 1524—printed in Nürnberg and Erfurt—give us a first look at the melodies that were provided for this early wave of hymn production. The title page of the 1524 collection of eight hymns *Etlich Cristlich lider* ("Some Christian songs") indicates "Wittenberg," but it was actually printed in Nürnberg. The lengthy title states that these hymns accord with the pure Word of God and the Holy Scriptures, are written by highly learned individuals, and are to be sung in church, as is the practice in Wittenberg. There are eight hymn texts in this collection, thus it is sometimes referred to as the "Achtliederbuch" ("eight songs book"). The first two hymns are "Dear Christians, One and All, Rejoice" (*LSB* 556) by Luther and "Salvation unto Us Has Come" (*LSB* 555) by Paul Speratus (1484–1551). Each of these two hymns

---

7   Robin A. Leaver, *The Whole Church Sings: Congregational Singing in Luther's Wittenberg* (Grand Rapids, MI: Eerdmans, 2017).

appears with notated melodies, the same melodies that we sing to-day: NUN FREUT EUCH and ES IST DAS HEIL, respectively. The melody for "Salvation unto Us Has Come" is reprinted thirteen pages later for Luther's paraphrase of Psalm 12, "Ach Gott, vom Himmel sieh darein" ("O Lord, Look Down from Heaven, Behold"; cf. text at *TLH* 260), and a heading at the top of that page states: "One sings the following three Psalms to this melody." Thus, the melody for "Salvation unto Us Has Come" serves four of the eight hymns in this early collection—Speratus's text of the same title, as well as Luther's three psalm paraphrases (Psalms 12, 14, and 130). Moreover, in two 1524 Erfurt hymnals from rival printers, each entitled *Enchiridion*, Luther's "Dear Christians, One and All, Rejoice" is coupled with the melody for "Salvation unto Us Has Come" rather than the NUN FREUT EUCH melody printed in the "Achtliederbuch" as the very first hymn.

At this earliest stage of hymnal printing, one can understand the apparent flexibility of how texts and tunes are connected, how one tune can accommodate several texts that all share the metrical scheme 87 87 887. Printers were scrambling to get hymn collections out to the public, for there was a market not only for the individually printed broadsides but also for collections of hymns written in connection with the newly emerging religious impulses and theological positions of the Reformation movement. If an Erfurt printer didn't need to engrave yet another tune, he could get his copies out for sale that much sooner.

Apart from such practical matters, interesting philosophical questions arise—at least for us at a later time as we consider questions of meaning in the music of early Lutheranism. What is clear is that there was not necessarily a one-to-one correspondence between tune and text in these earliest hymns (nor indeed in subsequent eras, including our own time). Thus, the pitches and rhythms of the melody—presumably written by Luther—for his text "Dear Christians, One and All, Rejoice" were not seen as a necessary condition for printing (or singing) that hymn text. It could just as well be sung to the melody for "Salvation unto Us Has Come," as shown in the Erfurt hymnal. Moreover, the tune that we know as ES IST GEWISSLICH (see *LSB* 508 and 693) was used as early as 1533 for "Dear Christians, One and All, Rejoice" (*LSB-CH* 1:585, 452).

What does all of this suggest regarding questions of meaning in music? Though in our time and place all Lutheran hymnals use Luther's tune NUN FREUT EUCH as found in the 1524 "Achtliederbuch,"[8] in the early sixteenth century, there was no one set of pitches and rhythms that *meant* or signaled "Dear Christians, One and All, Rejoice." The significant commonality among the three tunes—NUN FREUT EUCH, ES IST DAS HEIL, and ES IST GEWISSLICH—that supported Luther's text is that all three find their origins in the Church's own creative culture. The tune NUN FREUT EUCH is generally accepted as an original tune by Luther, matching his ten-stanza text of the same title. The tune ES IST DAS HEIL finds its roots in earlier German sources, the earliest dating from the late fourteenth century, connected to Easter texts (*LSB-CH* 1:583).

---

8   *TLH, LBW, LW, CW93, ELH, ELW, LSB,* and *CW21.* The same is true of the German hymnal *EG,* which uses NUN FREUT EUCH for Luther's text.

The tune we know as ES IST GEWISSLICH was coupled with Luther's "Nun freut euch" text in the 1533 Wittenberg hymnal *Geistliche lieder auffs new gebessert zu Wittemberg* ("Spiritual songs newly revised for Wittenberg"). Significantly, in the 1545 hymnal *Geystliche Lieder* ("Spiritual songs"), printed in Leipzig by Valentin Babst and including a preface by Luther, both tunes are provided for Luther's text: the ES IST GEWISSLICH melody printed first as no. XXXII (see Example 2), followed by three pages containing all ten stanzas of text, followed by the NUN FREUT EUCH melody printed as no. XXXIII (see Example 3). Clearly, at this point, both tunes were considered appropriate for singing this text.

This 1545 hymnal, often referred to as the "Babst Gesangbuch," was published one year before Luther's death and was the last hymnal to include a preface by Luther. In this preface, he again alludes to the proclamatory aspect of music and singing:

> For God has cheered our hearts and minds through his dear Son, whom he gave for us to redeem us from sin, death, and the devil. He who believes this earnestly cannot be quiet about it. But he must gladly and willingly sing and speak about it so that others also may come and hear it. (AE 53:333)

The believer cannot be quiet but "must gladly and willingly sing and speak." Why? "So that others also may come and hear it." That is a powerful reminder for us as we gather on a weekly basis for God's Divine Service to us. He gives us His Word, forgives us our sins through a called and ordained pastor, and gives us His

Example 2

Example 3

very body and blood "under the bread and wine" (*LSB*, p. 326) for the forgiveness of sins. In response to these gifts, we praise God "with both word and music, namely, by proclaiming [the Word of God] through music" (AE 53:323). So when we sing a hymn like "Dear Christians, One and All, Rejoice," we are not just "singing doctrine," as some would have it. On the contrary, we are proclaiming the Word of God, which is the chief way we praise God for His goodness to us. And as we "willingly sing and speak," others in our assemblies "come and hear" this good news of redemption "from sin, death, and the devil." The Babst hymnal of 1545 shows us that either tune—ES IST GEWISSLICH or NUN FREUT EUCH—was deemed appropriate to support and complement Luther's text; either tune could convey the meaning of Luther's hymn text.

Over time, however, associative musical meanings might change a bit. Growing up with *TLH*, I assumed that the tune we know as ES IST GEWISSLICH was always linked to that same text: "Es ist gewisslich an der Zeit" ("The Day Is Surely Drawing Near"; *TLH* 611; *LSB* 508). Thus, as a young organ student, I couldn't figure out why Bach's exuberant, sprightly organ chorale prelude on NUN FREUT EUCH (BWV 734) was based not on that tune but on the ES IST GEWISSLICH tune, which I associated with the judgment/end times hymn "The Day Is Surely Drawing Near." The naïveté was mine, of course, but that example does illustrate changing associations between music and text over time, with corresponding implications for the associative meanings inherent in hymn melodies. Bach, too, understood this hymn as one for end times, and notably in his cantata BWV 70, *Wachet! Betet! Betet! Wachet!*

("Watch! Pray! Pray! Watch!"), used a solo trumpet to sound the hymn melody in a particularly striking section of the cantata where the recitative text very effectively sounds both Law and Gospel, final judgment, and God's great compassion for sinners. Though the text of the chorale "Es ist gewisslich an der Zeit" was not sung by soloists or choir, the trumpet sounding the melody would have been sufficient for Bach's listeners, the trumpet melody signaling the text of this end times chorale within the Church Year context of a cantata for the Twenty-Sixth Sunday after Trinity.

As we saw in the 1524 "Achtliederbuch," it was not uncommon for one tune, ES IST DAS HEIL, to serve several texts. The same is true for our hymnals today, which underscores the fact that the pitches and rhythms that make up a hymn melody do not necessarily constitute or signal a theological meaning unique to a single text. For example, in *LSB*, the tune NUN FREUT EUCH is used for three hymns in addition to Luther's "Dear Christians, One and All, Rejoice": "On Christ's Ascension I Now Build" (*LSB* 492); "If Your Beloved Son, O God" (*LSB* 568), which at its 1630 publication was coupled with the tune of the Gloria hymn ALLEIN GOTT IN DER HÖH (*LSB-CH* 1:613); and Jon Vieker's (1961–) masterful translation "All Christians Who Have Been Baptized" (*LSB* 596) of Paul Gerhardt's (1607–76) Baptism hymn, which at its 1667 publication was coupled with the tune ES IST DAS HEIL (*LSB-CH* 1:679). And that tune is used twice in *LSB*: once in its accustomed place for the text "Salvation unto Us Has Come" (*LSB* 555) and again for another Baptism hymn, "All Who Believe and Are Baptized" (*LSB* 601).

This same kind of flexibility, where one strong tune can aptly convey the meaning of more than one text, is apparent in our time as well. Herbert Brokering (1926–2009) wrote the Easter hymn "Alleluia! Jesus Is Risen" (*LSB* 474) specifically for David N. Johnson's (1922–87) tune EARTH AND ALL STARS, originally composed for Brokering's text of the same title (*LSB* 817). Similarly, Carl Schalk's wonderful melody THINE was composed for Brokering's text "Thine the Amen, Thine the Praise" (*LSB* 680) but also serves very well in *LSB* as the setting for Stephen Starke's (1955–) Sanctus paraphrase in Divine Service, Setting Four (*LSB*, p. 208).

Summary

Luther's plan for the people to "sing during mass" became a hallmark of Lutheran worship—then and now. Hymn melodies are not only the most important music in the Lutheran Divine Service but also the most concise. Sometimes there is a one-to-one relationship between text and tune, where the tune has been wedded to that text alone, for example, HERZLICH LIEB for Martin Schalling's (1532–1608) text "Herzlich lieb hab ich dich, o Herr" ("Lord, Thee I Love with All My Heart," *LSB* 708). But often a hymn melody does not have a single meaning by virtue of being aligned with a single text. In cases where a hymn melody such as NUN FREUT EUCH or EARTH AND ALL STARS is wedded to more than one text, such hymn melodies often work very well to convey the meanings of separate texts that nevertheless share some significant overall traits in terms of theological emphasis. On the other hand, meanings can change over time, with the melody ES IST GEWISSLICH being a case in point: in our day being wedded to the end times text of that same title, "The Day Is Surely Drawing Near," rather than to Luther's magnificent text "Dear Christians, One and All, Rejoice."[9] What has worked best for tunes to signal theological meaning is when those melodies come out of the Church's own creative culture, though judicious borrowing from Western art music (for example, the hymn tunes by Isaac, Hassler, and Holst mentioned in the previous chapter) has given the Church melodies that have taken on new meanings within the Church's sung proclamation.

---

9   *LSB*, like *TLH* before it, also assigns this tune to the text "O Holy Spirit, Grant Us Grace" (*TLH* 293, *LSB* 693).

CHAPTER 3

MUSIC FOR VOICES AND INSTRUMENTS IN THE LUTHERAN SERVICE: WHAT DOES IT MEAN?

I began this inquiry into meaning in Lutheran music by considering hymn tunes and how they signal and convey theological meaning. While hymn tunes are the most concise musical elements in the liturgy, they are also, arguably, the most important since hymns are the primary means by which a congregation proclaims the Gospel and sings the faith. Of course, hymn tunes have composers, who consider a hymn text and then imagine appropriate pitches and rhythms to accommodate and convey that text, always considering that this music will be sung by the congregation—an assembly of singers who may or may not read music from the printed pages of the hymnal, and who may or may not have any vocal training or experience other than singing in church. A hymn melody needs to have a certain intuitive, inevitable quality about it, which enables the congregational singer to grasp the tune readily. And yet good hymn tunes are never simplistic. In the face of these realities, crafting a hymn melody is not an easy task. We admire these concise musical expressions by some of the Church's finest composers, ranging from Luther (1483–1546) himself and Philipp Nicolai (1556–1608) in the sixteenth century, to Johann Crüger (1598–1662) in the seventeenth century, to Carl Schalk (1929–2021) in the twentieth and twenty-first centuries.

As we have seen in the two previous chapters, hymn tunes do signal and convey meaning, but because there is not necessarily a one-to-one relationship between a given melody and a single text, musical meaning in hymn tunes becomes a flexible proposition. In our time, these tune/text relationships are determined in part by the committees that put together our hymnals, for once a hymnal or hymnal supplement has been published, congregational singers will find themselves the heirs of either well-conceived or poorly conceived unions of hymn melodies and hymn texts—poor unions being situations where the meaning that the hymn melody conveys is not a suitable complement to the meaning of the text. Meaning in hymn tunes is not only a function of composers, or of publishers (like Babst in 1545), or of twenty-first-century hymnal committees; it is also a *learned* understanding by us as congregational singers, who grow up in, or become part of, a particular Lutheran culture, assimilating the liturgical and hymnic substances of that culture, with the result that certain meanings, including those of Lutheran hymnody, become deeply embedded.

But when we move beyond hymn melodies to consider more extended compositions of Lutheran music—whether for voices, instruments, or both—questions of meaning are somewhat different. Composers find ways to build meaning into their more extended compositions in ways that are not possible with the concise nature of hymn tunes. Furthermore, a single melody most often accommodates multiple stanzas of poetic hymn text, often with multiple strands of meaning. So while I can assert fairly that Nicolai's hymn tune WIE SCHÖN LEUCHTET *signals primarily* his text "O Morning Star, How Fair and Bright," or that Ralph Vaughan Williams's (1872–1958) hymn tune SINE NOMINE *means* "For All the Saints Who from Their Labors Rest," those associations are established by tradition and *learned* by us as congregational singers and listeners—*not* because of compositional means employed in these concise melodies. But the situation may be different when a composer turns to more extended forms of vocal/choral or instrumental music for the Lutheran worship service. Sometimes we can readily hear and see how the composer builds theological meaning into a particular work. At other times in vocal/choral or organ music, musical meaning is an *associative* prospect, where a hymn melody signals meaning, and where the composer shapes music that not only appropriately complements a particular theological text (for example, a hymn text) but also enhances and heightens the meaning of that text through music.

As we go beyond hymn tunes, two composers will loom large in this discussion: the great Lutheran kantors Michael Praetorius (1571–1621) and Johann Sebastian Bach (1685–1750), both of whom devoted much of their lives to music for the Church. We gain insights to musical meaning not only from a composer's body of musical works but also from a composer's prose writings, from historical circumstances relating to specific church-related duties, or from the intended functional placement of the music within the liturgies of the composer's own time and place.

MICHAEL PRAETORIUS

When we think of notable composers of music for the Lutheran Church, it is perhaps predictable, and certainly understandable, that J. S. Bach is most often the first to come to mind. We likely hear his music in our worship services more often than that of his early-seventeenth-century precursor Michael Praetorius, though Praetorius's harmonization of the melody ES IST EIN ROS is heard frequently at Christmas, whether sung by a choir or by the congregation (see "Lo, How a Rose E'er Blooming," *LSB* 359). What is most remarkable about Praetorius is his prolific output of chorale-based compositions. His nine-part series of publications entitled *Musae Sioniae* ("Muses of Zion"), published during the years 1605 to 1610, contains more than 1,200 harmonizations, as well as extended compositions on the German chorale repertory (including that well-known setting of "Lo, How a Rose"). What makes these volumes such a treasure is not only the sheer quantity of compositions but also the musical variety, ranging from straightforward harmonizations of chorales to elaborate settings for more than one choir.[10]

Unlike many composers, Praetorius was also a prolific writer *about* music, publishing three of a projected four volumes of his encyclopedic treatise on music, *Syntagma Musicum*.

---

10   For an overview of Praetorius and his work, see Carl Schalk, *Music in Early Lutheranism: Shaping the Tradition 1524–1672* (St. Louis: Concordia Academic Press, 2001), 93–113.

Volume one (1615), written in Latin and intended for the clergy, was a historical and philosophical treatise on sacred music. Volumes two and three, written in German and intended for musicians, covered musical instruments (volume 2, 1618/19) and music theory broadly defined (volume 3, 1619). A fourth volume, on composition, unfortunately never came to fruition. As both composer and theorist, Praetorius was amazingly industrious and has bequeathed to us a body of work second to none in the history of Lutheran music.

As we consider meaning in Lutheran music, we don't expect that composers such as Praetorius or Bach will tell us in explicit prose what their music means. They were busy writing music for the Church, often on a weekly basis; they had no reason to ask the kind of reflective questions that I pose here as a way of thinking about how Lutheran music signals and conveys theological meaning. And yet, Praetorius, more than most composers, did reflect on music in the Lutheran liturgical service—not precisely on "what does this mean?" but nevertheless on ways that music should work in the theological context of Lutheran worship. His thoughts, written down in Part One of the first volume of *Syntagma Musicum*, have implications for this inquiry on meaning in Lutheran music.[11]

On the very first page of Part One, Praetorius asserts:

> Two occupations are required for the complete and finished perfection of the divine liturgy, as it is carried out at the public gatherings of the

---

11   A partial translation from Latin to English of *Syntagma Musicum*, Part One, is found in PraeSM I.

church, namely, speech and song. (PraeSM I, 4)

Here Praetorius uses the similar sounding Latin words *concio* (speech) and *cantio* (song). A few pages later, he insists that within Lutheran worship, speech and song are fully equal partners, that both exist on the same plane. He writes the following for Lutheran pastors:

> So should those entrusted with the supervision of the church completely avoid ever separating or pulling apart speech and song in the ecclesiastical system of the public liturgy. . . . The perfect and complete liturgy consist of two duties, that is, speech and song. (Prae-SM I, 7)

Praetorius stresses, moreover, that the content of speech and song must be identical:

> Speech and song preach and celebrate the doctrine of the same confession of Christ, and of the propitiation made by his blood. . . . The confession of the adorable Triune is most gloriously celebrated in heart and voice by the consonance of teaching and singing. (PraeSM I, 10, 11)

While he is not posing or answering the question "What does this [music] mean?" he ascribes to music in Lutheran worship the same function as preaching. Both sermon (speech = *concio*) and music (song = *cantio*) preach Christ, justification through His blood, and the confession of the triune God. Clearly, for Praetorius, music is a vehicle for proclaiming the same theological content as may be heard in the sermons of Lutheran pastors. In that sense, the sacred music of the liturgy, like the sermon, has a kind of exegetical function in which explanation, interpretation, and commentary on Scripture are expected.

He is even more explicit about the content of the music itself in what he calls the "liturgy of preaching and singing":

> The music adopted by our churches from the primitive churches in psalms, responsories, hymns, antiphons, etc., sings only of that which is consonant with the preaching of the Prophets and the Apostles . . . exactly in agreement with Holy Scripture, and varying [but] little from it. (PraeSM I, 18; brackets in original)

Throughout the opening section of this first volume of *Syntagma Musicum*, Praetorius is constantly looking back at the history of the Church's music, at what the Fathers of the Church had to say about "the liturgy of speech and song"—thus his emphasis on how the music of the Early Church was "exactly in agreement with Holy Scripture." For example, Praetorius quotes Justin Martyr (ca. 100–ca. 165): "For it is the Word of God, whether thought with the mind, or sung, or played on an instrument" (PraeSM I, 19). Praetorius finds in Justin Martyr a precedent for equating speech and song, sermon and music, as equal partners in the liturgy, for—as stated so succinctly by Justin—it is all the Word of God.

Apart from insisting on the scriptural content of "the liturgy of speech and song," he comments briefly on his work as a composer, "arrang[ing] and harmoniz[ing] . . . German hymns by Luther and others," as well as "arrang[ing] for choirs of voices, organs, and other instruments, Latin songs in the style of motets, for the entire liturgical year" (PraeSM I, 20). Just as Luther wished to retain the Latin Mass—so that the young could learn the Latin language while still having the people sing in their own language—Praetorius responded by composing Latin music for the liturgy as well as settings of German-language hymns (chorales). His regard for the musical heritage of the Church is noteworthy: "I always make a great effort when setting sacred hymns, to regard with one eye the choral melody used by the church, and with the other, my own harmony" (PraeSM I, 21). One can take this to mean that he essentially set some boundaries for himself as a composer. Whether the basis for his composition is a chorale melody or Latin chant, he keeps "one eye" on that preexistent musical material even while he "adorn[s] it and present[s] it in many guises" (PraeSM I, 21). By taking that compositional approach, he enhances the *associative meaning* of those compositions so that the listener can perceive the chorale melody even as the composer adorns it with new music. In this way, the listener is enabled to recall the theological meaning of the text as it is *signaled* by Praetorius's musical setting. Few composers of the early seventeenth century (still the first century of the Lutheran Church) did this as well as Michael Praetorius. There is a certain humility about his approach as a composer for the Church, one that could well be emulated by the Church's musicians in our day:

If someone wishes to sing in church, he should sing

with the church. Nor do I wish to have anyone counted among the musicians who, in undertaking any task for the church, totally disregards the accepted norms of choral melody in church, who sets himself up to indulge only his own taste and temperament. (Prae-SM I, 20–21)

In my introductory comments concerning the purpose of this book, I wrote that it is intended for the singers and listeners of Lutheran congregations. Praetorius is also concerned with the acts of singing and listening, and by implication, with the fact that music, like preaching, is a vehicle that conveys theological meaning:

Certainly a mind [possessed] of devout faith perceives that in choral music and the psalmody of the church, the glory of God has been spread about. For indeed [choral music] balances, considers, and reflects on the importance of each word and sentence, and presents them for contemplation to the alert singer and the aroused listener. (PraeSM I, 61; brackets in original)

Here Praetorius is addressing meaning in Lutheran music. When music "presents" "each word and sentence" "for contemplation" by the "aroused listener," music is, in fact, conveying and signaling theological meaning. The composer, in this case Praetorius, has so "adorned" the preexistent chorale melody that the listener's senses are aroused to receive the music as a heightened form of theological meaning.

LISTENING: If "the proof of the pudding is in the eating thereof," then proof of the power of Praetorius's music is in the listening thereof, and I encourage the reader to listen to the recording of Praetorius's *Mass for Christmas Morning* as reconstructed by Paul McCreesh and Robin A. Leaver (released on the Deutsche Grammophon Archiv label in 1994, with the manufacturer's label number of 439 250-2, which is, unfortunately, no longer available for purchase). This recording is, however, available on YouTube; search for "Mass for Christmas Morning." This listening experience will illustrate as no other can how Praetorius's music is the *cantio* that stands next to the Christmas morning *concio*, speech and music combining to convey the good news of the incarnation of Christ as Savior of the world.

JOHANN SEBASTIAN BACH

Bach's music for the Divine Service includes organ preludes on Lutheran chorales as well as cantatas for voices and instruments. Bach rarely used the term "cantata," instead usually referring to the "*Hauptmusik*" ("the principal music") of the Divine Service, which occurred most often after the reading of the Gospel and before the sermon—the principal music/cantata thus functioning as the musical counterpart to the sermon (or, in Praetorius's words, the *cantio* before the *concio*). "Cantata" is a term used during Bach's lifetime (particularly in Italy) to designate a multimovement composition for voices and instruments, and from the mid-nineteenth century became the term used most frequently for this significant body of Bach's works for voices and instruments, which was intended for specific Sundays in the Church Year or other occasions such as funerals. In addition to organ chorales and cantatas, Bach also contributed passion settings for Good Friday, notably the monumental settings of the *St. John Passion* and the *St. Matthew Passion*. All three of these genres (organ chorale preludes, cantatas, passion settings) have received a great deal of scholarly attention, focusing in part on how Bach's music reflects and proclaims the theological meaning inherent in the texts—the chorale texts of the organ music and the biblical and chorale texts found in the cantata and passion librettos, as well as the poetic texts that paraphrase and reflect on biblical truths and Lutheran confessional norms in both cantatas and passions.

My focus in this book, of course, is not primarily on Bach—his biography, career, and music—but on the overarching question of meaning in Lutheran music. Accordingly, I will look at three organ chorale preludes, one cantata, and the opening chorus of the *St. Matthew Passion* to illustrate how Bach conveyed theological meaning through his music. No composer has ever done so more consistently, brilliantly, or beautifully.

Bach: Organ Chorale Preludes

During his years at the ducal court in Weimar (1708–17), Bach worked primarily as an organist, adding to those duties from 1714 the obligation to compose one cantata per month for the court chapel. One of his organ-related projects during the Weimar years was his *Orgelbüchlein* ("Little Organ Book"), a manuscript in which Bach laid out—page by page—the titles of 164 Lutheran chorales he proposed to set for organ. He composed directly into this manuscript and completed 46 of the proposed chorales. On the title page of his manuscript, Bach stated two specific pedagogical goals for this collection: how the organist can (1) learn to compose or improvise an organ setting of a chorale in various ways and (2) increase his skills in pedaling—since each of Bach's settings was written with an independent pedal part that could not be omitted or transferred to the left hand. But beyond such didactic intentions, the collection clearly has a practical use in providing organ settings for use during the Church Year; in fact, the collection is organized by Church Year, beginning with Advent and extending through Christmas, the New Year, Lent, Easter, Ascension, Pentecost, and Holy Trinity, before moving to chorales without a specific Church Year assignment. One imagines that some of these brief compositions might well have been used by Bach to introduce the singing of a chorale in the Weimar court chapel.

Bach's setting of the chorale "Durch Adams Fall ist ganz verderbt" ("Through Adam's fall everything is corrupted") has often been included in anthologies of music scores for historical study. Thus, the undergraduate music history student becomes acquainted with this brief composition as emblematic of Bach's organ chorale preludes. But why this piece? Because here Bach very effectively uses a series of falling intervals in the pedal part—sevenths that are dissonant within the overall harmonic context—to symbolize Adam's fall into sin. It's a brilliant compositional choice that keeps reminding the listener (twenty-four times!) throughout this brief piece that this music is about Adam's *fall* into sin. Bach's very literal pictorial compositional choice thus portrays or pictures the fall into sin, the basis of original sin (see Psalm 51:5). Bach's organ setting conveys specific meaning, not only by having the chorale melody sound very perceptibly in the upper voice of the musical texture, but also by the reiterated falling sevenths in the lowest voice of the texture. Both are perceptible, and both signal meaning for the listener.

LISTENING: Bach's chorale prelude is available on You-Tube in several performances; search "Durch Adams Fall" or "Bach BWV 637."

By choosing this particular composition, I run the risk—as do textbook anthology editors—of suggesting that all of Bach's chorale preludes will behave similarly, thus inviting the listener essentially "to go on a picture hunt" in any given organ chorale prelude. But, of course, Bach isn't so literal all, or even most, of the time. Often it is a more subtle approach. For example, in the Christmas chorale prelude "Der Tag, der ist so Freudenreich" ("Hail the Day So Rich in Cheer," *TLH* 78), Bach places an insistent, continuous rhythmic motive in the left hand, while the right hand presents the hymn melody very clearly, and the organist's feet play a continually moving bass line, including some striking descending scale passages. That striding bass line coupled with the constant rhythmic activity of the left hand makes the whole feel rather dancelike and suggests and underscores the sense of joy occasioned by the birth of the Savior.

LISTENING: Listen to this organ setting on YouTube by searching either "Bach Freudenreich" or "Bach BWV 605."

By contrast, in his setting of the passion chorale "O Mensch, bewein dein Sünde gross" ("O man, bewail your grievous sins"; cf. *ELH* 272), Bach uses musical means to express sorrow for sins—so pervasive that only the death of God's Son could pay the price. Of course, the composer can't "picture" sin or sorrow in a literal way (as was the case with Adam's "fall"), but through various musical means, he makes it possible for the listener to recognize the theological realities of this hymn text, especially the sinner's sorrow over sins committed (see 1 John 1:8–9). He does so in part by specifying a slow tempo for this composition, by elaborating the hymn melody so intensely as to nearly mask recognition of the melody, and by providing a rich harmonic context for this heavily ornamented melody. (Music historians might speak of "chromaticism" in this composition, meaning that Bach's melodic elaboration and use of harmony goes well beyond the musical norms of, for example, a hymn harmonization in one of our hymnals.)

LISTENING: Listen to this organ setting on YouTube by searching either "Bach bewein organ" or "Bach BWV 622."

Meaning in Bach's *Orgelbüchlein* chorale preludes, and indeed in his more extended organ chorale settings, invites our careful listening, but it is rarely as clearly pictorial as it is in "Durch Adams Fall." Still, the point is that Bach was a master at filling his organ settings with meaning, from the associative meaning of a clearly projected and perceptible chorale melody to the kinds of rhythmic, melodic, and harmonic means found in these examples from his brief but brilliant settings in the "Little Organ Book." They are little in length but great in meaning!

BACH: *GOTTES ZEIT IST DIE ALLERBESTE ZEIT* (BWV 106)

For an example of how Bach conveys meaning in the music of a cantata, I turn now to an early cantata by Bach, *Gottes Zeit ist die allerbeste Zeit* ("God's time is the very best time").

LISTENING: It will be essential to listen to this work before reading what follows here. Searching YouTube by either the proper German title ("Gottes Zeit ist die allerbeste Zeit") or the popular subtitle of this work ("Actus tragicus") will bring up a choice of performances.

For convenience, here is the text and translation of this cantata:

Gottes Zeit ist die allerbeste Zeit.
God's time is the very best time.
"In ihm leben, weben und sind wir," solange er will.
"In Him we live, move, and have our being,"
as long as He wills. [Acts 17:28]

In ihm sterben wir zur rechten Zeit, wenn er will.
In Him we die at the right time, when He wills.

Ach, Herr, "lehre uns bedenken, daß wir sterben müssen,
auf daß wir klug werden."
Ah, Lord, "teach us to consider that we must die,
so that we become wise." [Ps. 90:12]

"Bestelle dein Haus; denn du wirst sterben
und nicht lebendig bleiben!"
"Set your house in order, for you shall die
and not remain living!" [Is. 38:1]

"Es ist der alte Bund:" Mensch, "du mußt sterben!"
"It is the old law:" Man, "you must die!" [Sirach 14:17]
"Ja, komm, Herr Jesu!"
"Yes, come, Lord Jesus!" [Rev. 22:20]

"In deine Hände befehl ich meinen Geist; du hast mich
erlöset, Herr, du getreuer Gott."
"Into Your hands I commit my spirit; You have
redeemed me, Lord, You faithful God." [Ps. 31:5]

"Heute wirst du mit mir im Paradies sein."
"Today you will be with Me in paradise." [Luke 23:43]

Mit Fried und Freud ich fahr dahin
in Gottes Willen,
getrost ist mir mein Herz und Sinn,

sanft und stille,
wie Gott mir verheißen hat:
Der Tod ist mein Schlaf worden.

> In peace and joy I now depart
> According to God's will.
> Confident is my heart and mind,
> Calm and still.
> As God has promised:
> Death has now become my sleep. [cf. *LSB* 938:1]

Glorie, Lob, Ehr und Herrlichkeit
sei dir, Gott Vater und Sohn bereit,
dem Heilgen Geist mit Namen!
Die göttlich Kraft
macht uns sieghaft
durch Jesum Christum, amen.

> Glory, praise, honor, and splendor
> Be given to You, God the Father and Son,
> And to the Holy Spirit by name!
> May the power of God
> Make us triumphant
> Through Jesus Christ, amen. [cf. *LSB* 734:5]

This cantata, likely composed for a funeral—perhaps that of Bach's uncle Tobias Lämmerhirt, who died on August 10, 1707—is usually dated to the time of Bach's work as organist in Mühlhausen, 1707–08, thus when Bach was 22–23 years of age. We don't know the identity of the person who compiled the text of this cantata. Perhaps it was one of the pastors in the town of Mühlhausen, perhaps Pastor Georg Christian Eilmar, who was godfather to Bach's first daughter. The text is largely a series of biblical passages, skillfully connected by small additions of free text. The Bach scholar Renate Steiger identified a seventeenth-century printed precedent that provided a model for combining biblical and chorale texts—the *Christliche Bet-Schule* (the "Christian School of Prayer") by Johann Olearius, published in Leipzig in 1668.[12] Thus, the text compiler of *Gottes Zeit ist die allerbeste Zeit* was not working in a vacuum but rather drawing on an established tradition of devotional and prayer literature that pulled together related biblical passages and chorale texts for specific occasions (not unlike what the *Treasury of Daily Prayer*[13] provides for us today).

This early cantata consists of a series of relatively short textual and musical sections, rather like the cantatas of Dieterich Buxtehude (ca. 1637–1707), whom Bach had visited in Lübeck during a four-month period in late 1705 and early 1706. It is not surprising that only a year-and-a-half later Bach would still have that type of cantata very much in his ears and in his consciousness.

After the initial statement that "God's time is the very best time," the text moves to parallel statements on living and dying. The first of these sections is based on a phrase taken from Acts 17:28: "In Him we live and move and have our being," to which

---

12 Renate Steiger, "Actus tragicus und ars moriendi: Bachs Textvorlage für die Kantate 'Gottes Zeit ist die allerbeste Zeit' (BWV 106)," *Musik und Kirche* 59 (1989): 11–23; "J. S. Bachs Gebetbuch? Ein Fund am Rande einer Ausstellung," *Musik und Kirche* 55 (1985): 231–34.

13 *Treasury of Daily Prayer* (St. Louis: Concordia Publishing House, 2008).

the anonymous text compiler has added "as long as He wills." The parallel statement on dying is free text, that is, not quoted from a biblical source: "In Him we die at the right time, when He wills." To illustrate the meaning here, Bach sets the second of these two sections ("In Him we die") at a suddenly slower tempo and with much half-step chromatic movement to underscore the word "*sterben*" ("we die").

The text of the next section is based on Psalm 90:12: "So teach us to number our days that we may get a heart of wisdom," though the German in the cantata text is more specific: "Ah, Lord, teach us to consider *that we must die*, so that we become wise" (emphasis added). The subsequent section is based on a portion of Isaiah 38:1: "Set your house in order, for you shall die, you shall not recover." To this point, the anonymous text compiler has reminded listeners that our time for living and our time for dying are in God's hands. The two passages from Psalm 90 and Isaiah 38, then, serve as further reminders that we will, in fact, die. Thus far, our anonymous text compiler is preaching the Law, preaching that the consequence of sin is death.

The next section of the cantata begins by repeating that same theme, quoting from the apocryphal book of Sirach 14:17: "for the decree from of old is, 'You will surely die!'" To symbolize the ancient decree, the Law, Bach writes a three-part fugal exposition, fugue being a strict musical procedure that functions according to musical laws. He uses the alto, tenor, and bass voices for this three-part fugal exposition, the soprano not entering until sixteen measures into this fugal section. When the soprano voice does enter, the listener realizes that suddenly everything has changed, for the soprano enters with a new text and breaks free musically from the strict fugue that has thus far been the essence of this section. At this pivotal moment in Bach's cantata, the soprano sounds the first note of Gospel. From Revelation 22:20, the soprano's text is "Yes, come, Lord Jesus!" As the soprano continues to repeat this text, the instruments (two recorders and two violas da gamba) begin to provide their own theological commentary—the third layer of meaning in this musical section—by sounding the chorale "Ich hab mein Sach Gott heimgestellt," which signaled to Bach's listeners the text (at least the first stanza) of that chorale:

> I have commended my things to God;
> He does with me as He pleases.
> If I am to live still longer here,
> I do not resist.
> I submit to His will.

As the first phrase of this chorale is completed in the instruments, the three-part fugue in alto, tenor, and bass resumes—after all, the Law is with us until the end of time. But so, too, does the soprano return with the same text: "*komm, Herr Jesu*." Law and Gospel are thus superimposed in Bach's musical texture, with the Gospel occupying the highest pitch level. The Law continues its insistent course in the lower voices, but the voice we hear most prominently points us to Christ, and that is sheer Gospel. While one could read this and understand it from the written text, Bach uses these layers of music to heighten the meaning of the text. The instruments continue to play the chorale—phrase by phrase, the chorale text attesting to the believer's submission to God's will; after all, His time is the very best time. Bach ends this extraordinary movement in the most remarkable way: after the lower three voices have asserted for the final time "man, you must die," the soprano continues on with one final, elaborate "*Herr Jesu*," ending the movement by herself, on the word "*Jesu*," with no other instrument or voices participating. Bach has used musical means to point the listener to the Gospel, to Christ, who fulfilled the Law to save us. We hear the Gospel alone sounding at the end of this pivotal section in Bach's cantata.

Given that the Gospel has the final word in that section of the cantata, what is the response of the believer? The next section begins with the alto singing Psalm 31:5: "Into Your hand I commit my spirit; You have redeemed me, O LORD, faithful God." This prayer of the Christian is then answered by the bass singing the words that Jesus spoke on the cross to the penitent thief crucified alongside Him, from Luke 23:43: "Truly, I say to you, today you will be with Me in paradise." (In his passion settings, too, Bach uses the bass voice to sing the words of Jesus.) As Bach emphasizes the words "in paradise," the alto returns, now singing the chorale "Mit Fried und Freud ich fahr dahin" ("In Peace and Joy I Now Depart"), a paraphrase of the Nunc Dimittis. Thus, in this movement, the believer commits his soul into God's hands, and Jesus proclaims that today the believer (identified by the pronoun "*du*," the familiar "you" in German) will be with Him in paradise. The believer responds by

73

singing the paraphrase of the Nunc Dimittis, Jesus all the while continuing to sing His words of comfort, until the last lines of the chorale: "Calm and still. / As God has promised: / Death has now become my sleep."

In each of the two sections discussed here at length, Bach (and his text compiler) provide *layers of meaning*. In the first instance, two texts are superimposed, one representing Law and the other Gospel, while the instrumental forces sound a chorale that provides yet a third layer of related meaning. In the second instance, Christ's words of Gospel promise evoke a response from the believer, which is stated in the text of a well-known chorale. Only because Christ has paid the full price for sins, and promised paradise to penitent sinners, can the believer die in peace and joy, confident, calm, and still, knowing that death is a sleep from which he will be awakened on the Last Day to enter bodily the heavenly dwelling that Christ Himself has prepared. The listener grasps these layers of meaning by filtering Bach's musical procedures through an understanding of and familiarity with Lutheran theology.

Bach concludes the cantata with a doxological stanza from the chorale "In dich hab ich gehoffet, Herr" ("I Trust, O Lord, Your Holy Name," *LSB* 734), with special emphasis on the last line of the chorale stanza, "*durch Jesum Christum, amen,*" a concluding Christological emphasis reminding the listener that Christ is indeed the key to the theological meaning of this entire text. The Bach scholar Alfred Dürr aptly summarized this cantata as "a work of genius such as even great masters seldom achieve. Here, in one stroke, the twenty-two-year-old composer left all his contemporaries far behind him. Of course, it could be argued that in later years Bach's art became a great deal more mature, but it hardly grew more profound."[14]

BACH: *ST. MATTHEW PASSION* (OPENING CHORUS)

The *St. Matthew Passion* dates from Bach's Leipzig years, 1723–50, and was probably first performed on Good Friday, April 11, of 1727. The magnificent opening chorus provides another example of how Bach employs a specific Lutheran chorale to signal meaning. This chorus is scored for orchestra and three groups of singers—two four-part vocal ensembles and a third group of soprano voices, in Bach's day a boys' choir, that sings the melody of the chorale "O Lamm Gottes, unschuldig" ("Lamb of God, Pure and Holy," *LSB* 434).

LISTENING: Here again a search of YouTube, using "Bach St. Matthew Passion," will bring up a choice of several performances, thus allowing the reader to hear this opening chorus before considering what follows here.

The first of the four-part vocal ensembles begins by singing: "Come, you daughters, help me lament." The second of the ensembles then poses questions that are answered by the first ensemble.

Ensemble 1: "See"
Ensemble 2: "Whom?"

---

14   Alfred Dürr, *The Cantatas of J. S. Bach*, rev. and trans. Richard D. P. Jones (Oxford: Oxford University Press, 2005), 759.

Ensemble 1: "The Bridegroom"

Ensemble 1: "See"
Ensemble 2: "How?"
Ensemble 1: "As a lamb"

As if to clarify matters, the third group of singers (the soprano voices) then enters with the chorale text and melody, which was well known to Bach's Leipzig listeners, and is, in fact, still commonly sung in many Lutheran congregations during midweek Lenten and Holy Week services. The chorale makes clear that the Bridegroom, the Lamb, being lamented is Christ, the innocent, guiltless ("*unschuldig*") Lamb of God. The two four-part ensembles continue:

Ensemble 1: "See"
Ensemble 2: "What?"
Ensemble 1: "The patience"

To which the third and fourth lines of the chorale enter as a kind of commentary (in the *LSB* translation): "Ever patient and lowly, Thyself to scorn didst offer."

Ensemble 1: "Look"
Ensemble 2: "Where?"
Ensemble 1: "To our guilt"

But again the chorale enters, announcing the remedy for our guilt and bearing a word of Gospel:

All sins have You borne
Otherwise we must give up hope.

(or, in the words of the *LSB* translation:)

> All sins Thou borest for us,
> Else had despair reigned o'er us.

The questions of the second four-part ensemble having been answered, those two ensembles join in singing the closing lines of this chorus:

> See Him who out of love and grace
> Bears the wood of the cross.

Simultaneously, the sopranos sing the final line of the chorale: "Have mercy on us, O Jesus!" Bach uses this well-known chorale, sung by a separate and distinct choir, to clarify the Christocentric meaning of the opening chorus. Thus, this opening chorus of the *St. Matthew Passion* effectively summarizes all that is to come in Matthew's detailed account of our Lord's passion: the guiltless One dies in place of the guilty ones—all of us.

SUMMARY

When the church composer engages in a more extended musical work—as opposed to a hymn melody—there is, of course, greater opportunity to build meaning into the music, as Bach does, for example, in his cantata *Gottes Zeit ist die allerbeste Zeit* or in his organ setting of "Durch Adams Fall." For the composer, the extended piece, like a cantata or organ chorale prelude, is analogous to an artist painting on a larger canvas instead of working on a miniature. There is simply more space for the artist, more time for the composer, to infuse meaningful details that convey or enhance a theological narrative. And yet the concise, "miniature" form of a hymn melody remains a powerful signal for meaning, as is clear in the cantata BWV 106, in the opening chorus of the *St. Matthew Passion*, or in the clearly perceptible melody of the *Orgelbüchlein* setting of "Durch Adams Fall." The ear perceives these hymn melodies and associates the melody with the poetic text and then with the theological content of that text (melody → text → theology). That kind of associative meaning, which depends very much on known hymn or chorale melodies, is front and center in the chorale-based music of Praetorius and indeed in his understanding of how music (*cantio*) functions meaningfully in parallel with speech (*concio*) in the Divine Service, a foundational concept for Lutheran music that was articulated very clearly by Luther himself: "After all, the gift of language combined with the gift of song was only given to man to let him know that he should praise God with both word and music" (AE 53:323).

Word and music, speech and song, *concio* and *cantio*. Music draws its meaning from the word but then enhances and heightens that word in a musical proclamation of the Gospel that stands in parallel with the spoken proclamation of the Gospel. Both must be done with the greatest skill, which is why pastors hone their preaching abilities and musicians their singing and playing abilities, their compositional and improvisational skills—all in service of the Gospel.

CHAPTER 4

LITURGY, CHURCH YEAR, AND LECTIONARY AS CONTEXTS FOR MEANING

Let's return for a moment to Bach's cantata *Gottes Zeit ist die allerbeste Zeit* (BWV 106). Where might we hear this cantata sung live today, as opposed to a recorded performance on YouTube or elsewhere? It is highly unlikely that we will hear this cantata sung at a funeral in one of our churches. Moreover, it is certainly rare in North American Lutheran churches for a cantata to be sung after the Gospel and before the sermon at a Sunday Divine Service, thus emulating the regular practice in Bach's Leipzig. It is more likely in our time and place that one might occasionally hear a Bach cantata sung in the context of a Vespers or Evening Prayer service, whether in a church or at an academic institution—seminary or university—perhaps once a month, or on a seasonal basis during, say, the Advent or the Easter season. Or we might hear a cantata sung as part of a choral concert by a collegiate choir and instrumentalists. But we almost never encounter one of Bach's cantatas in its historical liturgical context. We know why—the musical forces needed simply are not readily available to most congregations. Bach himself acknowledged the demands of his cantatas when he wrote to the Leipzig town council in 1736 that "the concerted pieces [music for voices and instruments, i.e., cantatas] that are performed by the First Choir [of his students from the St. Thomas School], which are mostly of my own composition, are incomparably harder and more intricate than those sung by the Second Choir."[15] That level of difficulty for vocalists and instrumentalists is part of the reason why we rarely hear the cantatas of Bach, or other seventeenth- and eighteenth-century composers, in the Sunday Divine Service, at least in North America.

But when we do hear a cantata, BWV 106 for example, in the context of Vespers or in a concert, the meaning that Bach infused in this music, in part through the use of chorales as signal devices, is still present. I'll call that kind of meaning *inherent meaning*—the composer has built it into the music, and the meaning is present regardless of the performance occasion or venue. If this particular cantata were to be sung/played as part of a funeral liturgy, it would take on additional meaning, which I will call *contextual meaning*. Similarly, the cantata BWV 70, *Wachet! Betet! Betet! Wachet!* ("Watch! Pray! Pray! Watch!"), mentioned in chapter 2, would take on additional contextual meaning when sung/played in the Divine Service for one of the last Sundays of the Church Year, where it would be heard in the context of a Gospel reading and sermon proclaiming the ultimate comfort of the end times through the promise of eternal life in the presence of Christ. Put another way, one would be glad to hear this cantata in a concert, but how much

15   *The New Bach Reader: A Life of Johann Sebastian Bach in Letters and Documents*, ed. Hans T. David and Arthur Mendel, rev. and enl. Christoph Wolff (New York: Norton, 1998), 176.

greater would be the meaning in the appropriate liturgical, Church Year, and lectionary context, where the music (*cantio*) fully complements the spoken word (*concio*), the *integrated whole* being decidedly more beneficial theologically than its separate parts. This chapter will consider the prospect of an integrated whole, where musical meaning is dependent on the conjunction not only of spoken word (*concio*) and music (*cantio*) but also on the integration of music within the contexts of liturgy, Church Year, and lectionary—the contextual factors identified at the end of chapter 1.

MUSIC AS AN INTEGRATED PART OF THE DIVINE SERVICE: TWO VIEWS FROM THE NINETEENTH CENTURY

The possibility of music being a fully integrated part of the Divine Service is envisioned by Praetorius in his discussion of *concio* and *cantio*, and accomplished by Bach in his composition of cantatas as the "principal music" for each Divine Service in the Church Year. In an 1835 letter from the composer Felix Mendelssohn Bartholdy (1809–47) to Pastor Ernst Friedrich Albert Baur, we see Mendelssohn wrestling with the concept of music being integrated into the liturgy of his time:

> Genuine church music, i.e., for the evangelical Divine Service [*Gottesdienst*], which finds its place in the course of the churchly ceremony, seems to me impossible, and to be sure, not merely because I do not see completely *which* place in the Divine Service music should fit into, but rather because I cannot even think

in general of this place. Perhaps you have something to say to me, that makes it clearer to me, but up to now I do not know . . . how we can make music an integrated [*integrirender*] part of the Divine Service, and not merely a concert that stimulates devotion to a greater or lesser extent.[16]

Mendelssohn was unwilling to settle for music that would function merely as a concert within the Divine Service, that is, music that could not be well integrated within a liturgical context. Moreover, he was keenly aware that the Divine Service required its own *sacred* music—distinctive in style from the music of secular entertainments like opera. In this same letter, Mendelssohn criticized music composed for the Roman Catholic Mass by composers such as Francesco Durante (1684–1755) and Giovanni Battista Pergolesi (1710–36), who, in Mendelssohn's view, introduced "laughable little trills" ("*die lächerlichsten Trillerchen*") into their settings of the Gloria in Excelsis, as if it were a finale from an opera.

Later in the nineteenth century, the Lutheran pastor and seminary professor Friedrich Lochner (1822–1902), who was born and educated in Germany but moved to the United States in 1844 to serve as a Lutheran missionary, would also comment on the idea of music being well integrated in the Divine Service. He did so in

---

16   Felix Mendelssohn Bartholdy, *Sämtliche Briefe*, Bd. 4 (Kassel: Bärenreiter, 2008), 140–41: Eine wirkliche Kirchenmusik, d.h. für den evangelischen Gottesdienst, die während der kirchlichen Feier ihren Platz fände, scheint mir unmöglich, und zwar nicht blos, weil ich durchaus nicht sehe, an *welcher* Stelle des Gottesdienstes die Musik eingreifen sollte, sondern weil ich mir *überhaupt* diese Stelle gar nicht denken kann. Vielleicht hast Du mir etwas zu sagen, das mich darüber klarer macht, aber bis jetzt weiß ich nicht . . . wie es zu machen sein sollte, daß bei uns die Musik ein integrirender Theil des Gottesdienstes, und nicht blos ein Concert werde, das mehr oder weniger zur Andacht anrege (author's translation); emphasis in original.

his seminal work on the Lutheran liturgy, *Der Hauptgottesdienst der evangelisch-lutherischen Kirche* (St. Louis: Concordia Publishing House, 1895).[17] Specifically with regard to choral music in the Divine Service, Lochner wrote:

> Yet while choral singing is to occupy an *independent* position in the Divine Service in accordance with its significance indicated above, this should not be an *isolated* position, if the choir is to serve rightly in edifying the congregation and do its part in truly beautifying the Divine Service. The music which it performs must thus be *integrated* as closely as possible with the actions of the liturgist and the congregation so that choral singing does not appear as a performance or assume the character of a religious concert—which it certainly should **not**.[18]

Sixty years later than Mendelssohn, Lochner, too, was concerned that the music of the Divine Service not take on the characteristics of a performance or a religious concert. How to avoid that circumstance? By purposely and deliberately *integrating* the music with other aspects of the Divine Service.

Why cite Mendelssohn and Lochner in this discussion? Because it is critical to see that the goal of music being well integrated in the Divine Service is by no means a novel idea or a recently conceived agenda. From Luther and Praetorius—and their emphasis on the

---

17 English translation: Friedrich Lochner, *The Chief Divine Service of the Evangelical-Luthera Church*, trans. Matthew Carver, ed. Jon D. Vieker, Kevin J. Hildebrand, and Nathaniel S. Jensen (St. Louis: Concordia Publishing House, 2020).

18 Lochner, 31; emphasis in original.

close connection of "word and music" (Luther), "speech and song" (Praetorius)—to these two nineteenth-century calls for "integration" of music in the Divine Service, this hallmark characteristic of Lutheran music is clear. (And it might not be a stretch to include Bach's reference to "a well-regulated church music, to the glory of God," [19] though he never defined precisely what he meant by that phrase.) Returning for a moment to the quotation from Nicholas Cook at the very beginning of this book, if we believe that music in Lutheran worship should, in fact, be more than "just something nice to listen to," then integration of Lutheran music into the very fabric of the liturgy, in part via Church Year and lectionary, is a critical factor in how music takes on meaning in Lutheran worship.

Liturgy—The Divine Service

Music in Lutheran worship resides within—finds its meaning within—the liturgical contexts, or framework, of the Divine Service, as well as three daily Office, or prayer, hours: Matins (Morning Prayer), Vespers (Evening Prayer), and Compline (Prayer at the Close of the Day). Our focus here is on the Divine Service, or the Mass. In chapter 2, I referred to Luther's 1523 *Formula Missae*, his conservative revision of the Latin Mass. There Luther acknowledged that the liturgy of the Mass, as it had developed gradually from antiquity through the medieval period, was worthy of retention—with the exception of any elements that made the Mass into a sacrifice:

---

19   Bach uses this phrase twice in his 1708 request to be released from his position as organist in Mühlhausen; see *The New Bach Reader*, 57.

We therefore first assert: It is not now nor ever has been our intention to abolish the liturgical service of God completely, but rather to purify the one that is now in use from the wretched accretions which corrupt it and to point out an evangelical use. . . . But in this book we are not going to prove again that the mass is neither a sacrifice nor a good work—we have amply demonstrated that elsewhere. We do accept it as a sacrament, a testament, the blessing (as in Latin), the eucharist (as in Greek), the Table of the Lord, the Lord's Supper, the Lord's Memorial, communion, or by whatever evangelical name you please, so long as it is not polluted by the name of sacrifice or work. (AE 53:20, 22)

Luther goes on to praise the Early Fathers of the Church who participated in the gradual process of adding elements to the liturgy of the Mass. Indeed, the history of the Mass is in part a history of additions to a basic liturgical pattern dating back at least to the middle of the second century.

Justin Martyr (ca. 100–ca. 165), in his *Apology*, described a Sunday service with the Lord's Supper, identifying the following components:

- Readings (from the Prophets and the Apostles)
- Sermon
- Prayers

- Lord's Supper
  (Bread and wine brought, prayers and thanksgiving over the elements, people speak "Amen," distribution of bread and wine to the people)

Thus, according to Justin's account, a gathering of Christians in the mid-second century would have been based around Word and Sacrament. Additions to this basic pattern took place over centuries, with the fourth-century Edict of Milan (313), which paved the way for Christians to engage in their distinctive patterns of worship without fear of persecution, providing a new level of freedom for development of the Christian Church, including its ritual patterns.

The Mass as it developed from the fourth through approximately the seventh century was fully defined long before Luther would have encountered it. He took great care in the *Formula Missae* to identify those parts of the Mass that met with his approval:

- Introit
- Kyrie eleison
- Gloria in Excelsis
- Collect
- Epistle
- Gradual
- Alleluia

- Gospel
- Nicene Creed
- Sermon
- Preface
- Words of Institution
- Sanctus
- Lord's Prayer

- Agnus Dei
- Communion chant
- Collect
- Benedicamus Domino ("Bless we the Lord")
- Benediction

There is a wonderful continuity in the liturgy of the Mass from the second century to our present day. Were Justin Martyr able to observe our Divine Service, he would see that its large-scale structure continues to be defined by Word and Sacrament, as was the Christian gathering that he documented circa 150. Were Luther able to observe our Divine Service, he would recognize the close parallels to the fully developed Latin Mass of the late Middle Ages, as well as the conservative reforms of his *Formula Missae* (1523).

Lutheran Service Book (2006) provides five settings of the Divine Service, all of which are structured identically around three major components: Confession and Absolution, Service of the Word, and Service of the Sacrament. This large-scale structure recognizes that Christ comes to us with His gifts of forgiveness of sins, His Word, and His very body and blood in the Sacrament of His Holy Supper. The Divine Service is quite literally where the Divine "serves us" with His gifts, which subsequently elicits our praise and thanks. God's gifts to us are primary; our praise is secondary and prompted by receiving His good gifts. See, for example, the Offertory text on page 159 of *LSB* (Setting One):

> What shall I render to the Lord
> > for all His benefits to me?
> I will offer the sacrifice of thanksgiving
> > and will call on the name of the Lord. [Ps. 116:12–13]

God's gifts ("His benefits") come first; our response follows ("I will offer the sacrifice of thanksgiving").

If one compares the five settings of the Divine Service in *LSB*, one sees immediately that there is (intentionally) a good deal of musical variety among these settings. There is some textual variety as well. Setting Four, for example, employs hymn-based paraphrases of the Gloria in Excelsis, the Sanctus, and the Agnus Dei. But the overall framework is consistent. Not only do all settings of the Divine Service share the three major components—Confession and Absolution, Word, Sacrament—but even within those components, there are consistent overall patterns, including (1) texts that are the same every time we gather (Ordinary texts) and (2) texts that are different each time (proper texts, meaning "proper" to a particular Sunday or festival). Again, with reference to *LSB* Setting One: the Kyrie (pp. 152–53), the Hymn of Praise—Gloria in Excelsis (p. 154) or "This Is the Feast" (p. 155)—the Sanctus (p. 161), and the Agnus Dei (p. 163) are the sung Ordinary texts of the *LSB* Divine Service (the Hymn of Praise being omitted in Advent and Lent). Proper texts in the Divine Service include the following:

Introit, Psalm, or Entrance Hymn	p. 152
Old Testament or First Reading	p. 156
Psalm or Gradual	p. 156
Epistle or Second Reading	p. 156
Alleluia and Appointed Verse	p. 156
Holy Gospel	p. 157

The Ordinary portions of the Divine Service (Kyrie, Gloria, Sanctus, Agnus Dei) are sung by the congregation. The musical propers of Introit, Gradual, and appointed Alleluia Verse are sung by the choir or kantor. Additionally, hymns—notably an Entrance Hymn and the Hymn of the Day (pp. 152, 158)—are sung by the congregation.

Thus, music is built into the liturgy of the Divine Service, at times for the congregation, at times for a choir or kantor. Moreover, additional musical elements are sometimes introduced into this overall framework: for example, a prelude, perhaps based on one of the hymns; a vocal/choral motet or anthem, perhaps sung during the offering; additional hymns, organ music, or vocal/choral music sung during distribution of the Lord's Supper; a closing or recessional hymn. Whether musical ordinary or proper text, hymn, or additional instrumental or vocal/choral music, all music should find its place carefully integrated within the liturgy of the Divine Service. Two further contextual factors—Church Year and lectionary—also play defining roles in integrating music within the overall structure of the Divine Service.

CHURCH YEAR

The Church Year, or church calendar, provides a means of organizing time and, together with the lectionary, functions to define further a theological context in which music may take on specific meaning. On an annual basis, beginning four Sundays before Christmas, the Church Year immerses the Christian in the story of God's salvation for humanity.

Following the four-week period of preparation that is the season of Advent, the Church observes the incarnation of God's Son, the birth of the Savior, at Christmas. The season of Epiphany follows as the Church marks the manifestation of Christ to the Gentiles, the Baptism of Christ, and His first miracles. The season of Lent—forty days, excluding Sundays, from Ash Wednesday to Easter—is a time of repentance and preparation. During Holy Week, the Church remembers the passion of Christ, moving from His entry into Jerusalem on Palm/Passion Sunday, through Maundy Thursday and Good Friday, to the Vigil of Easter. Easter—the celebration of the resurrection of Christ and His defeat of death—is observed as a season of fifty days, extending from Easter to the Day of Pentecost. Within the Easter season, the Church observes the festival of Christ's ascension into heaven. Pentecost—the fiftieth day after Easter—marks the sending of the Holy Spirit, as Jesus had promised (John 15:26; Acts 1:8). Thus, this first portion of the Church Year enables us on an annual basis to recall the birth, Baptism, ministry, passion, death, resurrection, and ascension of Christ, together with the sending of the Holy Spirit, who "calls, gathers, enlightens, and sanctifies the whole Christian Church on earth, and keeps it with Jesus Christ in the one true faith" (Small Catechism, Third Article; *LSB*, p. 323).

The Sundays after Pentecost make up essentially the second half of the Church Year, sometimes referred to as the "Time of the Church," a rather imprecise term that we may understand as the time after the earthly ministry of Jesus, after His ascension into heaven, and the time before the parousia—the second coming of Christ, when Jesus will return in final judgment. Characteristic of the close of the Church Year, from November 1 (All Saints' Day) to the Last Sunday of the Church Year, is an emphasis on the end times.

LECTIONARY

If the Church Year is a way of organizing time, the lectionary is a way of providing specific biblical readings for every Sunday and festival of the Christian year. Both Church Year and lectionary provide an objective basis for preaching and teaching "the whole counsel of God" (Acts 20:27), an objective way of thinking theologically in the context of corporate worship. *LSB* provides both a three-year lectionary (*LSB*, pp. xiv–xix) and a one-year lectionary (*LSB*, pp. xx–xxi), both lectionaries specifying Old Testament, Epistle, and Gospel readings throughout the Church Year. Both Church Year and lectionary furnish a kind of guardrail against individual biases, favorites, hobby horses, or quirky creative impulses, providing instead an objective framework for proclamation of the Word.

The three-year lectionary designates one of the three Synoptic Gospels for each year: year A draws on Matthew, year B on Mark, and year C on Luke. Since Mark is shorter than the other two Synoptic Gospels, series B also draws on the Gospel of John. But John's Gospel is used in all three series, notably during the Easter season. The First Reading often connects closely with the Gospel for the day. While the First Reading is usually taken from the Old Testament, the Book of Acts is used during the Easter season. The Second Reading in the three-year lectionary is usually drawn from one of the New Testament Epistles (occasionally from Acts or

Revelation) and most often read in a continuous fashion over a series of weeks, thus giving opportunity to hear substantial portions of the Epistles within the span of three years.

For a case study of how the lectionary can focus meaning on a particular Sunday, let us consider Proper 21 in year C, which was the Sixteenth Sunday after Pentecost in 2022. The appointed Gospel is Luke 16:19–31, the story of the rich man and poor Lazarus. The appointed Old Testament reading, which complements the Gospel, is from Amos 6:1–7, where the prophet warns those who are rich and live a life of ease and excess against injustices and idolatry. Similarly, in the Gospel account, the rich man, who lived a life of ease and excess ("feasted sumptuously every day"), was oblivious to the needs of the poor beggar at his gate. When Lazarus died, he "was carried by the angels to Abraham's side," and the rich man went to Hades, with its concomitant torment and separation from God. Though in the three-year lectionary the Epistle does not necessarily connect with the Gospel and Old Testament readings, on this particular Sunday, there is a choice of two readings from 1 Timothy, the second of which (6:6–19) includes a warning against "the love of money," Paul urging instead "godliness with contentment." Thus, all three readings focus the listener's attention away from greed and the idolatry of riches and toward God, "who richly provides us with everything to enjoy" (1 Timothy 6:17). The appointed Psalm (146) also focuses our attention on the same theme. It is the Lord God "who executes justice for the oppressed, who gives food to the hungry," who "lifts up those who are bowed down." Thus, the lectionary—in all four of its readings—does its job of focusing listeners on a particular theme. Now the question for us is how *music* might underscore and contribute to that theme, music thereby taking on specific meaning for this Sunday in the Church Year.

Of course, the first musical consideration is hymnody—finding a hymn text (or texts) that can comment on, contribute to, and reinforce the thematic focus of the Scripture readings specified in the lectionary. In the Lutheran tradition, the hymn that comments most specifically on the predominant lectionary theme for a given Sunday or feast is known as the Hymn of the Day. It is the principal hymn in the Divine Service, positioned between the reading of the Gospel and the sermon (see, for example, *LSB*, pp. 157–58 or 190–92). For Proper 21 in year C, Martin Schalling's hymn "Lord, Thee I Love with All My Heart" (*LSB* 708) is an appropriate Hymn of the Day. In stanza 1, the phrases "Lord, Thee I love with all my heart" and "Earth has no pleasure I would share" counter seeking after earthly wealth, riches, and the ease that Amos the prophet railed against. Stanza 2 refers to the Lord's "rich bounty" in providing "body, soul, and all I have." We singers ask in the second stanza that we "glorify Thy lavish grace" and "help and serve my neighbor"—precisely the opposite of the rich man in the story Jesus relates. And then that marvelous third stanza—one of the great treasures of Lutheran hymnody! Schalling draws directly on the story of poor Lazarus: "The poor man died and was carried by the angels to Abraham's side" (Luke 16:22):

Lord, let at last Thine angels come,

To Abr'ham's bosom bear me home,

That I may die unfearing.

Here Schalling perhaps imagines what might have been a recurring prayer by the poor man in Jesus' story. Schalling's hymn text serves as an example of how the Hymn of the Day appropriately captures the scriptural focus of the lectionary readings for a particular Sunday in the Church Year. The four lectionary readings are closely connected with one another, and Schalling's hymn is the primary musical expression to be integrated to this larger whole.

Of course, beyond the Hymn of the Day, there are other musical possibilities to be integrated into the worship service on this particular Sunday. For example, the young J. S. Bach composed an organ prelude (BWV 1115) on Schalling's hymn, with the melody of the A section of this bar form chorale being readily perceptible in the first half of Bach's setting. One could easily imagine the young Bach using this setting to prepare his congregation to sing the chorale "Herzlich lieb hab ich dich, o Herr" ("Lord, Thee I Love with All My Heart"). It is a composition that could be well integrated as a prelude on the Sunday when Schalling's hymn text complements the readings so well, Bach's organ setting thus taking on specific meaning by way of its connection to the hymn melody and text.

LISTENING: Listen to Bach's organ setting on YouTube by searching "Bach BWV 1115."

More recently, Walter L. Pelz has provided a very accessible organ setting of this hymn, again with a readily perceptible reference to the hymn melody.[20] And Timothy Shaw has done the same in providing a setting for piano.[21] Such keyboard settings may be well integrated to the service as preludes precisely because they bear clear references to the chorale melody, thus allowing the listener to link the musical composition to the hymn text and ultimately to the readings for the day as well as the preaching. In this way, music plays its role in proclaiming the Gospel through a process of associative meaning.

Vocal and choral music for this particular Sunday might include a setting of Psalm 146 or perhaps Bach's harmonization of the chorale "Herzlich lieb hab ich dich, o Herr" (st. 3), which closes the *St. John Passion*. Such choices would be well integrated with the lectionary readings for this Sunday.

SUMMARY

For music to take on specific meaning within Lutheran worship, it must be well integrated into the liturgical parameters of the Divine Service, particularly as defined through the contexts of Church Year and lectionary. The lectionary provides an objective framework for choosing hymns as well as vocal/choral music that complements the readings. Subsequently, a hymn—both a poetic/literary and musical expression—provides a basis for choosing fur-

---

20   In *Lutheran Service Book: Hymn Prelude Library*, ed. Kevin Hildebrand (St. Louis: Concordia Publishing House, 2014), vol. 5, 40–41.

21   In *Lutheran Service Book: Piano Prelude Series*, ed. Kevin Hildebrand (St. Louis: Concordia Publishing House, 2020), vol. 5, 45–47.

ther instrumental music (hymn preludes) that fit well within the Divine Service and have the capacity to connect closely with other elements in the worship service. The continuum extending from lectionary readings → hymns and vocal/choral music → instrumental music enables all of these musical genres (e.g., hymns, organ preludes, choral motets and anthems) to take on meaning within the Divine Service. While a free work such as an organ prelude and fugue by Bach may be played as a prelude, it is not possible for such a work to be integrated into the larger theological context of the Divine Service in the same way that an organ chorale prelude may be so integrated. This distinction doesn't preclude the free organ work; it simply means that such a work may bear aesthetic meaning but not specific theological meaning.

CHAPTER 5

SINGING AND LISTENING IN THE DIVINE SERVICE

As a high school student just beginning to play the organ in church, I thought of the liturgy in purely pragmatic terms—it was the "order of service," which I reviewed closely each Sunday so that I would insert my musical obligations in exactly the right places. Eventually I learned that the liturgy is far more than an order of service. In the liturgy—the Divine Service, the Mass—God comes to His people in Word and Sacrament, delivering forgiveness of sins and eternal life. We saw that pattern described by Justin Martyr circa 150, and the fulsome Divine Service of our day may be traced back to Luther's 1523 reform of the Mass. This historic continuity of the Divine Service is worth emphasizing, for it shows us what the Church has always been about: proclaiming the Word and administering the Sacraments—the Means of Grace that are the very heart of the Christian Church.

A 2021 report on the Evangelical Lutheran Mission Diocese of Finland brings these striking words from the Rev. Risto Soramies, the outgoing ELMDF bishop: "Through much of the history of Finnish Christianity, we thought very little of the liturgy, and we thought that we could live without it. But we cannot."[22] We cannot live without the Divine Service because that is where God serves us with His richest gifts, gifts that carry us through the difficulties of this life by keeping us focused on the heavenly Sanctus (Revelation 4:8) and the eternal marriage supper of the Lamb (Revelation 19:9). In Revelation 4:8, we read of the four living creatures: "Day and night they never cease to say, 'Holy, holy, holy, is the Lord God Almighty, who was and is and is to come!'"

"They never cease to say" (or, RSV: "sing"). Those words apply to the Divine Service in our day, too, for Lutheran congregants are always *singers*. We are also *listeners*—to music within the Divine Service, as well as to biblical readings and the preaching of God's Word. While much has been written about the history of Lutheran music—liturgy, hymnody, vocal and instrumental genres of music—we don't know as much as we might like historically about how people actually participated in the Divine Service through active singing and attentive listening.

Social historian Tanya Kevorkian has studied Leipzig in Bach's day to glean information about how congregants in Leipzig churches participated in the *Hauptgottesdienst* (the principal Divine Service) on Sunday mornings. She writes that "hymns were often sung during home worship, and were internalized through repeated singing. . . . People sang the 16th century hymns written by Luther and other reformers by heart."[23] She notes further that by the 1710s, it was common for congregants to bring their

22   Kevin Armbrust, "To Live Is Christ," *Lutherans Engage the World* (Fall 2021): 9.
23   Tanya Kevorkian, *Baroque Piety: Religion, Society, and Music in Leipzig, 1650–1750* (Aldershot, UK: Ashgate, 2007), 37.

own hymnals to the Divine Service, and by the early 1730s, hymn numbers were posted on boards positioned around the churches.[24] Thus, there is evidence that congregants in Bach's Leipzig did indeed participate in *singing*.

In terms of *listening* to music in the Divine Service, Kevorkian focuses on cantatas, which would alternate between the two principal churches, St. Thomas and St. Nicholas. Bach would have his first choir sing a cantata at St. Thomas on one Sunday, then a different cantata at St. Nicholas the following Sunday, the cantata texts always keyed to the Epistle and Gospel readings appointed in the lectionary for each Sunday in the Church Year. Kevorkian's study notes "there are numerous signs that many congregants did pay attention to the music."[25] Among the evidence for close listening was the availability for purchase of small, printed booklets that would provide the full texts of cantatas for a group of several upcoming Sundays. Kevorkian notes that such relatively inexpensive booklets sold well, with congregants able to follow along with the texts for the Sunday cantatas, thus enabling attentive, informed listening.

One wonders what future historians might write about congregational singing and listening in Lutheran churches of the early twenty-first century, about how people took part in the Divine Service. Just as Kevorkian focused on one particular city and its principal churches, so, too, our imagined future historians will have to paint with a very fine brush in order to describe singing and listening during a time when both liturgical and musical practices

---

24   Kevorkian, 38.
25   Kevorkian, 41.

vary considerably from place to place or, within a single parish, even from one worship service to another on the same day of the Church Year. But having acknowledged that reality, some observations on singing and listening, and the meaning of music in the Divine Service of our time, are possible.

Singing

We live in an era when each of the major Lutheran church bodies in the United States has published a hymnal within the last twenty years:

The Lutheran Church—Missouri Synod
Lutheran Service Book (2006)
Predecessor: *Lutheran Worship* (1982)
Interim supplement: *Hymnal Supplement 98* (1998)

Evangelical Lutheran Church in America
Evangelical Lutheran Worship (2006)
Predecessor: *Lutheran Book of Worship* (1978)
Interim supplement: *With One Voice* (1995)

Wisconsin Evangelical Lutheran Synod
Christian Worship: Hymnal (2021)
Predecessor:
 Christian Worship: A Lutheran Hymnal (1993)
Interim supplement: *Christian Worship Supplement* (2008)

Each of these twenty-first-century Lutheran hymnals has its own emphases, to be sure, but one finds in all of them older chorales as well as newer hymnody, with a mix of poets and composers both from within and outside of Lutheranism. All three books consciously include hymnody of varying ethnic traditions as well. Each book also contains various liturgical orders: in *LSB*, five settings for "Divine Service"; in *ELW*, ten settings for "Holy Communion" and one for "Service of the Word"; and in *CW21*, three settings for "The Service." Each book also provides services for "Daily Office" (*LSB*) or "Daily Prayer" (*ELW* and *CW21*). The point here is not to compare the three volumes but simply to say that each hymnal provides a richly varied menu for congregational singing, oftentimes more than any one parish will explore even over several years.

Thus, riches for congregational singing are readily available. But completing the arduous work of planning, producing, and publishing a new hymnal is not the end of the story. Nor is service planning and the use of the hymnal by pastors and church musicians the end of the story. The very real work of hymnal production, and subsequent service planning, finds its culmination in the act of congregational singing. The urgent and necessary premise must be that congregational singers understand their active role in Gospel proclamation, which is the *raison d'être* for hymns and hymnals. For example, on the First Sunday in Lent, the Gospel tells us of Jesus being tempted by Satan in the wilderness. When we sing the Hymn of the Day "A Mighty Fortress Is Our God," we proclaim that even if devils were to fill all the world, they cannot harm us. Satan is, in Luther's words, "judged; the deed is done" (st. 3). We sing in order to proclaim that Gospel truth—to one another and to all who might be present in our assemblies. Similarly, on the

Second Sunday of Easter, the Gospel (John 20:19–31) tells us of Jesus appearing to the disciples, including Thomas, after His resurrection. When we sing the late-fifteenth-century text (translated as) "O Sons and Daughters of the King" (*LSB* 470/471), we use poetry and music to recount that scriptural narrative and to proclaim the resurrected body of Jesus—blessed are we who have not seen and yet believe. We sing hymns for a reason—to proclaim the Gospel. And we remember Luther's premise, too, that the way we praise God is by proclaiming the Word of God through music.[26]

There is another premise about singing that we twenty-first-century congregational singers need to keep in mind. Before we sing the Sanctus ("Holy, holy, holy Lord"), we hear these words: "Therefore with angels and archangels and with all the company of heaven we laud and magnify Your glorious name, evermore praising You and saying . . ." We hear these words so often that their startling claim may elude us. When we sing the Sanctus, we do so "with angels and archangels and with all the company of heaven," in other words, with all the saints. We do so with our loved ones who have died in the faith. Arthur A. Just Jr. explains more fully:

> What we must always remember when we go to the Lord's Supper is that we commune with Christ and that wherever Christ is, there is heaven. And this communion includes all the saints who have died and risen in Christ . . . and all the saints now living all over the world, and those still to come. After someone dies, it is good to think of them at the Lord's Supper,

---

26   AE 53:323.

knowing that as we commune here below at the table of the Lamb and sing His songs, we do join them since they are simultaneously communing at the marriage feast of the Lamb in His kingdom that knows no end, and singing the songs of the Lamb with angels and archangels. In Christ, in that great mystery of our union with Him, we are joined to all who are joined to Him.[27]

For Lutheran congregational singers, this is a reminder of the significance, and the meaning, of our singing. Not only do our hymns participate in Gospel proclamation, but our singing places us in that heavenly feast that is ours forever in Christ. Our singing in church is much more than we might commonly understand it to be, possessed of greater significance and meaning than we may typically assume.

LISTENING

Much writing and thinking about music begins not with listeners and the act of listening but with the role of the *composer*—one who creates music by imagining its sounds and then specifying (through musical notation) pitches, rhythms, harmony, and instrumental and/or vocal sounds. Subsequently, on the basis of musical notation, whether on paper or on a computer screen, music is brought to life by *performers*, for the sake of *listeners*. (Sometimes the composer doesn't notate the music, instead improvising—

---

27   Arthur A. Just Jr., *Heaven on Earth: The Gifts of Christ in the Divine Service* (St. Louis: Concordia Publishing House, 2008), 212–13.

composing in the moment—music that may never be written down, *improvisation* playing a significant role in church music, especially by organists.) Thus, one can think of a continuum expressed as composer → performer → listener. The composer creates music, the performer "learns" that music, and the listener takes it in as a kind of consumer.

One could flip this continuum by suggesting the following. A particular group of listeners, for example, Lutherans in the Divine Service, requires new music for newly written hymn texts. Then an organist, choir director, or kantor needs organ and choir settings to introduce and support those newly written hymn tunes. The composer is called upon to provide specific types of music prompted by the needs of listeners in a specific functional context—in this case, the Divine Service. That continuum may be expressed as listener + performer → composer. Of course, in this case the analogy breaks down a bit because the listeners in question—the congregation—are actually both singers (= performers) and listeners, occupying a musical role that finds no precise analog in the world of concert or entertainment music.

While we are singers in the Divine Service, we are also listeners to other musicians, both singers and instrumentalists, who rehearse carefully for their functional roles in the liturgy. These parish musicians include those who play organ or piano, choir directors, the singers in our choirs—whether adults or children—and those who participate in bell ensembles, as well as other instrumentalists. Just as we don't think a great deal about our roles as congregational singers (we just do it), we probably don't think much about our roles as listeners of music in the Divine Service either.

Given the typical composer/performer/listener continuum, music scholars have paid the least attention to listeners, though that has begun to change in the past several decades as musicological scholarship increasingly views music as a social phenomenon rather than as an isolated, separate, aesthetic experience—the concert hall as an aural museum. Thus, it might be helpful here to think a bit about various ways of listening to music and how music in the Divine Service entails a specific type of listening experience.

Apart from church and the liturgical context of the Divine Service, we may listen to music for diversion—something to help a lengthy task, like a long car ride or repetitive work, pass more quickly. We may listen to music as a source for gaining energy. Watching professional athletes warm up before a game, we see them wearing earbuds and imagine that their playlists provide lively music that motivates not only their pregame warm-ups but also their competitive mental states. Listening to music for sheer entertainment, whether at a live concert or via streaming media, is perhaps the most common type of listening. Sometimes listening to popular music finds an audience standing, moving to rhythms, perhaps singing along with heavily amplified performers. In other venues, with other types of music, listeners are seated and follow along quietly, being careful not to disturb the performers or fellow listeners. They may follow the plot of an opera and empathize with certain characters. Or they may engage in structural listening, making every effort to follow and understand the composer's musical ideas and their subsequent development. But that kind of listener may or may not always engage music at a deep, structural level; at another opportunity, that same listener may not make the intellectual effort to listen in that way, perhaps preferring to let the sound of the symphony orchestra just wash over them, simply enjoying beautiful melodies and sounds. Thus, our reasons for listening to music and our ways of engaging with music are immensely varied and depend on at least these factors: (1) the context for listening—where and under what circumstances, (2) the type of music, and (3) the mental energy that the listener wishes to expend in engaging with the music.

Listening to music in the Divine Service is a particular type of listening experience. It is not listening to music for the sake of music—as at a concert or within the privacy of one's own headphones—but listening to music as a means of Gospel proclamation. It is listening to music, engaging with music, *theologically*—in the fully integrated theological context of liturgy, Church Year, lectionary, and music. Such theological listening within the context of the Divine Service demands first and foremost that we simply recognize it as a possibility. Pastors and church musicians will work to plan integrated services where the music plays its part in complementing the hymns and lectionary readings. Listeners—or perhaps more accurately, "singer/listeners"—will listen to music attentively, recognizing that music, too, is part of Gospel proclamation.

Consider, as one example, organ (and piano) music within the service. Earlier I made the point that, since the seventeenth century in the German-speaking regions of Europe, the organ has been accorded a position of prominence in Lutheran worship. As then, so also now, the organ is ideally suited to undergirding, supporting, and encouraging congregational singing, in spaces large and small. Further, the varied sonic resources of the organ are controlled by a single musician, which, for some churches, could be an important economic consideration. Just as the Lutheran hymnals cited earlier in this chapter are rich in resources, so also is the Lutheran Church rich in living composers who use these hymnals as points of departure for instrumental and choral music. At a time of newly published hymnals containing hymns new and old, living composers have turned to writing organ music based on these hymns. For example, the *Hymn Prelude Library*, edited by Kevin Hildebrand and published in twelve volumes (Concordia Publishing House, 2012–17), contains a newly commissioned organ setting for each hymn tune included in *LSB*. Moreover, the settings tend to be accessible to organists of average ability. For churches that may not have an organ or organist, a similar series of piano preludes is in the process of publication, so that eventually there will also be a piano prelude for each hymn in *LSB*. These two hymnal-based prelude series are but two examples of living composers responding to current hymnals and hymns by writing hymn-based instrumental music that can be well integrated to the Divine Service. Of greatest importance for congregational listeners, these settings present the hymn melody clearly, thus enabling the listener to relate the music—perhaps a prelude at the beginning of the service—to a hymn that will be sung that day, proclaiming the Gospel appointed in the lectionary for that day. Such compositions enable and invite that unique mode of listening—theological listening, where the music is tightly integrated within the Divine Service, playing its part in Gospel proclamation.

THEOLOGY OF WORSHIP → THEOLOGY OF MUSIC

A Lutheran theology of worship emphasizes what is primary and of first importance: in the Divine Service, we receive God's richest gifts—forgiveness of sins and the assurance of eternal life in the very presence of Christ. In the waters of Holy Baptism, God "claims us as His own" (*LSB*, p. 268) and, in the words of the Small Catechism, "works forgiveness of sins, rescues from death and the devil, and gives eternal salvation to all who believe" (Baptism, Second Part; *LSB*, p. 325). In the Lord's Supper, we receive the true body and blood of Christ "under the bread and wine" for the "forgiveness of sins, life, and salvation" (Sacrament of the Altar; *LSB*, pp. 326, 327). The Word of God, which permeates the Divine Service, is "able to make you wise for salvation through faith in Christ Jesus" (2 Timothy 3:15). The Holy Spirit works through the Word: "The Holy Spirit has called me by the Gospel, enlightened me with His gifts, sanctified and kept me in the true faith" (Third Article; *LSB*, p. 323). In the Divine Service, through Word and Sacrament, God is the gracious giver of priceless gifts—forgiveness of sins, salvation, and eternal life. Those gifts from our merciful God are *primary*. We receive those gifts and subsequently offer our thanks and praise, which is *secondary*. This Lutheran theology of worship "puts first things first," emphasizing God's life-giving gifts to His redeemed creatures, rather than our acts of praise, which sometimes are mistakenly conceptualized as the sum total of worship.

This Lutheran theology of *worship* is the basis for a Lutheran theology of *music*. In this theological understanding of music, proclamation of God's saving Word through music is primary. Luther identified language and music as God's gifts to be used in conjunction with one another for proclaiming the Word of God. Moreover, Luther understood that we praise God by proclaiming His Word. Thus, all of our music making in the Divine Service— sung portions of the liturgy (whether by congregation, pastor, or choir), hymns, choral and vocal music, instrumental music based on hymns—has this extraordinary proclamatory function. As Norman Nagel observed in his introduction to *Lutheran Worship* (1982): "The rhythm of our worship is from him to us, and then from us back to him. He gives his gifts, and together we receive and extol them." Earlier in that same introduction, Nagel noted: "Music is drawn into this thankfulness and praise, enlarging and elevating the adoration of our gracious giver God" (*LW*, p. 6).

As the Lutheran theology of *worship* serves as the basis for a Lutheran theology of *music*, one can observe a significant parallel. In this theology of *worship*, the focus is squarely on God's gifts to His creatures. In this theology of *music*, the focus is squarely on the musical proclamation of God's Word, the good news of the Gospel. Just as Lutheran worship is not about us but rather about what God has done for us, so, too, Lutheran music is not about the musicians, or even about the aesthetic beauty of the music, but it is primarily the proclamation of God's Word and secondarily the creatures' sacrifice of thanksgiving (see Psalm 116:17). As Nagel wrote: "Music is drawn into this thankfulness and praise," and, we might add, music is drawn into the very proclamation of the Gospel—Luther reminding us that proclamation and praise are inextricably connected.

That a Lutheran theology of music is based on and grounded in this Lutheran theology of worship makes all the difference in terms of what music *means* in the Lutheran Divine Service. Music in Lutheran worship is not only about expressing joy, though that is a part of what music may accomplish within the varied contexts of liturgy, Church Year, and lectionary. Music in Lutheran worship is not merely an accompaniment to times of reflection or meditation, though that is a part of what music may accomplish within the contexts of liturgy, Church Year, and lectionary. Music—particularly by way of hymns, vocal/choral music, and hymn-based instrumental music—takes on specific theological meaning in Lutheran worship. That is a distinctive characteristic of Lutheran music, one that congregational singers and listeners do well to regard and understand, and one that Lutheran pastors and church musicians will always seek to nurture.

Summary

As mentioned in the preface, this book is meant particularly for congregational singers and listeners who gather each Sunday